Western Viewpoints
an anthology of western and cowboy poetry

Edited by Clark Crouch
Cover Photo by Bess Crouch

Western Poetry Publications
[An imprint of The Resource Network}
Woodinville, Washington

Publications by The Resource Network

Western Poetry Publications Imprint
Where Horses Reign, 2004
Sun, Sand & Soapweed, 2005
Western Images, 2007
Eight Viewpoints, 2009
Views from the Saddle, 2009
Harkin' Home, 2010
Thirty: poems from The Country Register, 2013
Rustic Ruminations, 2013
Western Viewpoints, 2014
Prairie Knights (in press)

Creekside Poetry Publications Imprint
Poetic Reflections At The Creekside, 2013

The contents of two earlier books, *Voices of the Wind* and *Reflections* (iUniverse, 2002 and 2003), are contained in *Rustic Ruminations* (above). All publications are available internationally through local and internet booksellers.

Western Viewpoints

General contents Copyright ©2014 by Clark Crouch
Cover photograph Copyright ©1927 by Bess Crouch
Individual Poems Copyright © as stated with each poem

All rights reserved. No part of this book may be reproduced or transmitted in any form by any means, graphic, electronic, or mechanical including photocopying, recording, taping, or by any information storage retrieval system, without written permission.

Information and Permissions
Western Poetry Publications
18200 Wood-Sno Rd NE
Woodinville, WA 98072

ISBN-13: 978-1495466076
ISBN-10: 1495466078

Preface

This is our second eclectic collection of western and cowboy poetry, an anthology featuring ninety-two poems authored, for the most part, in the traditional form favored by classic cowboy poets such as Charles Badger Clark, In effect, it is a virtual open mic in printed form presented by true friends of that genre. The poems they have created are such as one might expect to hear and appreciate at a modern cowboy gathering.

In these pages you will find poems about the best of the West and a few renegades from the viewpoint of sixteen contemporary western and cowboy poets. Each poet has his or her own interests and style and together they offer a broad view of our great American West of yesterday and today.

The cover photograph depicts the editor's brother, Alferd Crouch, as he prepared to rule the west at age 11 some eighty-seven years ago in 1927. Grandpa's single action Colt rests on his hip attesting to his authority while his angora chaps establish his social position above any robbers, renegades, rustlers, or rascals he might encounter in his adventures. He was ready to tackle the West and so are we.

Clark Crouch, Editor
Western Poetry Publications
Woodinville, Washington

February 2014

Contents by Author

Preface v
Contents by Author vii
Contents by Title xi

Bradfield, Larry
  The Sun's Last Rays 1
  Where the Blacktop Ends 2
  Ole Jack Cody 4
  He Knew This Day Was Comin' 5
  West Texas Boy 7
  The Tenderfoot & Nasty 9
  A Cowboy's Last Will 11
  Longing for Kate 13
  One Foot on the Porch 15
  Winter Comes 17
  Don't Play Well With Others 18

Bradfield, Larry & Crouch, Clark
  Modern Cowboys 20

Crouch, Clark
  Horse Trainer 21
  The Rancher and the Boy 22
  Inland Sea 24
  Cookie's Cuisine 25
  Advice to an Eight Year Old 27
  Duke Morrison 28

Dachstadter, Neal
  The River Flowed 29
  Cold Winter, Wyoming 31

Dickson, Steve
   Cherokee Gal *32*
   The Race at the Old County Fair *33*
   My Little Town *35*
   Buffalo Moon *37*
   Dakota Wind *39*
   Half Moon Pass *41*
   A Friend at the End of the Line *44*
   The Bronc Rider *46*
   Raja and His Chuckwagon Days *48*
   The Bullfighter *52*
   River of No Return *53*
   Country Woman *55*
   Big Hat *56*
   Dancin' In The Dust *59*
   The Old Timer *61*
   Trails End *62*
   Moonlight in Montana *63*
   Tom Horn *65*

Foster, Stephen
   The Circuit Preacher *68*
   Where the Green Grass Grows *70*
   My Forest Camp *72*
   What Would the Lone Ranger Think *74*

Fry, Delia J.
   Southwestern Sky *75*

Gustafson, Del
   Ghosts in the Mist *76*
   Cow Docs *77*
   Dust *77*
   Honest Herb *79*
   Cattle Drive *80*
   The Stranger *83*
   Wild Herds *85*

Kopelke, Lynn
   Dance With Me, Mister *86*

Losey, Harold
   Doused *88*
   Hey Country *90*
   Bunkhouse Porch *92*
   My Home *93*
   Bullfighter *95*
   Cowboy Heaven *96*
   Mariah *97*
   Branding *98*
   Aces Over Eights *99*
   Cowboy *101*

Love, Charli
   Here's to Sippin' Velvet *103*
   Rodeos Are His Home *104*

Matley, Susan
   You Listen To The Boss *106*
   Green Energy *107*
   Dust *109*
   Bleached Bones *110*

Meyer, Debra
   The Patch *112*
   Hard Candy Cowboy *114*
   Heartache and Pards *117*
   Wooin' the Mule *119*
   Horse Sense *122*
   The Right Lead *125*

Peterson, LTC Roy E.
   Writers of the Purple Sage *128*
   Tucson Sunday Morning *129*

Swearingen, Tom
   Dogies in Our Band *130*
   A Winter Pleasure Ride *132*
   The Mystery of Superstition Mountain *134*
   First Night in Arizona *136*
   Horses and Happiness *138*
   Blessed to be Western *139*
   Nightwind. Gentle Spirit, Noble Soul *141*
   When a Horse Hoof Hits the Ground *143*

Taylor, J. Wesley, Jr.
   Going to the Rodeo *145*
   A Texas Picnic *147*
   A New Land *149*

Weaver, Don
   Snake Oil *151*
   Joe Wilson *154*
   People of the Prairie *156*
   Cowboy Larry & Ol' Stick *157*
   The High Drive *162*
   The Ballad of Bill Paxton *168*

   Brief Bios *171*

Contents by Title

A Cowboy's Last Will 11
A Friend at the End of the Line 44
A New Land 149
A Texas Picnic 147
A Winter Pleasure Ride 132
Aces Over Eights 99
Advice to an Eight Year Old 27
Big Hat 56
Bleached Bones 110
Blessed to be Western 139

Branding 98
Buffalo Moon 37
Bullfighter 95
Bunkhouse Porch 92
Cattle Drive 80
Cherokee Gal 32
Cold Winter, Wyoming 31
Cookie's Cuisine 25
Country Woman 55
Cow Docs 77

Cowboy Heaven 96
Cowboy Larry & Ol' Stick 157
Cowboy 101
Dakota Wind 39
Dance With Me, Mister 86
Dancin' In The Dust 59
Dogies in Our Band 130
Don't Play Well With Others 18
Doused 88
Duke Morrison 28

Dust	78
Dust	109
First Night in Arizona	136
Ghosts in the Mist	76
Going to the Rodeo	145
Green Energy	107
Half Moon Pass	41
Hard Candy Cowboy	114
He Knew This Day Was Comin'	5
Heartache and Pards	117
Here's to Sippin' Velvet	103
Hey Country	90
Honest Herb	79
Horse Sense	122
Horse Trainer	21
Horses and Happiness	138
Inland Sea	24
Joe Wilson	154
Longing for Kate	13
Mariah	97
Modern Cowboys	20
Moonlight in Montana	63
My Forest Camp	72
My Home	93
My Little Town	35
Nightwind. Gentle Spirit, Noble Soul	141
Ole Jack Cody	4
One Foot on the Porch	15
People of the Prairie	156
Raja and His Chuckwagon Days	48

River of No Return *53*
Rodeos Are His Home *104*
Snake Oil *151*
Southwestern Sky *75*
The Ballad of Bill Paxton *168*
The Bronc Rider *46*
The Bullfighter *52*
The Circuit Preacher *68*
The High Drive *162*
The Mystery of Superstition Mountain *134*

The Old Timer *61*
The Patch *112*
The Race at the Old County Fair *33*
The Rancher and the Boy *22*
The Right Lead *125*
The River Flowed *29*
The Stranger *83*
The Sun's Last Rays *1*
The Tenderfoot & Nasty *9*
Tom Horn *65*

Trails End *62*
Tucson Sunday Morning *129*
West Texas Boy *7*
What Would the Lone Ranger Think *74*
When a Horse Hoof Hits the Ground *143*
Where the Blacktop Ends *2*
Where the Green Grass Grows *70*
Wild Herds *85*
Winter Comes *17*
Wooin' the Mule *119*

Writers of the Purple Sage *128*
You Listen To The Boss *106*

The Sun's Last Rays
~~ Larry Bradfield — ©2013 ~~

I leaned against the bunkhouse wall,
Soaked up the sun's last rays.
Remembered when I never thought
There'd be an end to days.

I didn't know that I'd get old
And slow down in my gait.
It came on sudden-like it seems,
It's creepin' up of late.

I guess them broken bones don't help,
Or muscles torn apart.
This punchin' cows ain't for the weak,
Or for the faint of heart.

I think about the olden days,
At least olden to me -
I wish that I could live again,
And change what needs to be.

There was a love in Abilene,
Seems like I could have saved.
There were some paths I could have skipped -
Stayed on the roads that's paved.

But leanin' up against this wall,
About to close my eyes,
Seems 'bout as good as it can get -
No point in bein' wise !

Where the Blacktop Ends
~~ Larry Bradfield – ©2013 ~~

Out yonder where the blacktop ends
And precious moments start
Lives a broke down , wore out cowboy
Suff'rin' a broken heart.

Don't see him in the town no more,
Keeps mostly to hisself.
Don't talk about his plans these days.
He's put them on his shelf.

She was a beauty – no doubt there -
But that was long years past.
Don't seem to matter none to him,
He's mostly just downcast.

Well that's what hearts is for said he,
To pump blood and get broke.
He thinks that them's the truest words
The old man ever spoke.

I'd seen him bust a bronc' or two,
And rassle steers all day.
Tough as a boot he was, no doubt,
He dang shor' earned his pay.

Then along came this blonde haired gal
And he changed overnight.
He combed his hair and shaved his beard
And came home 'fore daylight.

Things went so well he thought he'd wed
That gal and say his vows.
Didn't know that she had eyes on
His boss that owned them cows.

So she became a rancher's wife,
And to her wealth she tends.
Now he's a crusty ole galoot,
Out where the blacktop ends.

Ole Jack Cody
~~ *Larry Bradfield – ©2013* ~~

Pull on your boots, ole Jack Cody,
The river's risin' fast.
Pull on your boots, ole Jack Cody,
The drought is broke at last!

Ain't rained a drop since five years gone,
The tanks has long been dry.
Grass been dead for a long, long time,
No use in wonderin' why.

His wife left near a year ago,
Girlfriend was close behind.
Sold his cows when the windmill broke,
Ain't nothin' on his mind.

Never said Texas was easy -
But I'll grant this is tough.
Just startin' over now and then
Takes about all your stuff.

But this here piece of real bad luck -
Looks like it's 'bout over.
Instead of watchin' sandstorms blow,
'Bout to plant some clover !

So get your hat, ole Jack Cody,
Come out and smell that rain.
Ain't nothin' quite as healin' as
Storms rollin' 'cross the plain.

He Knew This Day Was Comin'
~~ Larry Bradfield — ©2013 ~~

Where's it written he'd like to know,
That he must be a man.
He likes the way things are right now,
Doin' the best he can.

He turned thirteen last Friday morn,
And Pa gave him that look.
Like he could wear a bigger hat -
As if that's all it took.

He knew that day was comin' soon
When he'd put on the spurs.
He'd join the ranch hands at their chores
And fight the cockle burrs.

But dang he'd miss the life he's had -
It came and went too quick.
He'd cleaned up Texas pretty good
When his hoss was a stick.

He'd ride from daylight until dark -
His senses all alert.
He knew he'd bring outlaws to ground,
And cover them with dirt!

But that's about to end he knew.
He sighed and shook his head.
He'd have to let the outlaws go
And learn to rope instead.

Well, maybe there'd be good in this,
He'd shor' give it a whirl.
He knew that things was changin' fast -
He'd noticed some cowgirls!

There was a feelin' that he had -
Outlaws was easy stuff.
But catchin' girls looked kinda hard,
In fact just downright tough!

And, dang, he'd miss the life he had,
But he'd do what he could.
All he could say about them gals -
"This better shor' be good"

West Texas Boy
~~ Larry Bradfield – ©2012 ~~

They will bury my bones one of these days
On that windy ridge where the Mustang plays
It'll be time by then and time well spent
Not much I regret but some I'll repent

The first things I saw as a wee young lad
Were mesquite and sand and other things bad
My pa said money was scarce as could be
And rain didn't exist for folks like me

The dust bowl passed and the depression eased
All of a sudden folks seemed to be pleased
With my fam'ly and friends and jobs and such
Our homestead survived though not by too much

We roped and branded and paid off the note
On a plot of land full of creosote
Then to Odessa for a beer or two
Then went back to work, we had things to do

We had fences to mend and wells to dig
We had to repair the old drillin' rig
Calvin' time was about a month away
But they could start droppin' just any day

And then one day it all changed forever
A young man came by who was more clever
Than any of us ever claimed to be
He said where we lived was an ancient sea

He said that out of all this great nation
You've settled in the Permian Basin
You may not see it for a little while
But the oil 'neath your feet will make you smile

And so it came to be over the years
We still worked hard but shed a lot less tears
An oil well's pumping each quarter mile
They been doin' that for a long, long while

We're rich enough to buy them fancy boots
But we all remember our Texas roots
The mesquite and sand and the dust bowl years
Our young'uns work hard but with fewer fears

There's lots of outsiders don't like our state
Doin' lots of criticizin' of late
There's just one side to the story I see
The Lone Star State has shore been good to me !

The Tenderfoot & Nasty
~~ Larry Bradfield – ©2012 ~~

"Well, lookey here !" Bob said with glee
"We've got a tenderfoot !
He's got this brand new gear , you see
He don't know where to put"

"He says he comes from way Back East
Teach him a thing or two
Let's put him on that unbroke beast
And see what he can do"

The hoss they gave him don't look mean
Though Nasty was his name
He did seem sometimes really keen
On makin' riders lame

It seemed so like an awful match
New guy on this terror
This plot somehow just didn't hatch
We all judged in error

The greenhorn climbed upon that hoss
A move as slick as rain
He spurred to show him who was boss
And let him have the rein

Now Nasty gave him all he had
He bucked and whirled and screamed
The rider smiled, said "This ain't bad !
It's nothin' like I dreamed."

That hoss gave up, plum' tuckered out
The rider just stepped down.
Bob said "The East you lied about!
You've rode before this town !"

The new guy said, "Not in the least.
This here's New Mexico.
The whole of Texas lies Back East
I do believe it's so !"

They called him tenderfoot no more
He made a real smart hand
He came from Texas that's for shore
And that ole boy's got sand

A Cowboy's Last Will
~~ Larry Bradfield – ©2012 ~~

The old cowboy struggled for breath
Heartbeat faint, his eyes set,
He whispered softly before death
"Wait ! I ain't finished yet !"

"Don't lay me where my feet are cold
Or where the lightnin' plays
Keep me from rushin' waters bold
And where the rattler stays.

"Don't put me where they might stampede
I've seen enough of that
Or where the cliff face might recede
I'd rather see it flat.

"Keep me from where the Norther blows
And ice grows on your chin
I've seen enough of sleet and snows
And brutal killin' wind.

"And most of all protect me well
From sandstorms in my face
I'd rather face the fires of hell
Than sand in my last place.

"I know I'd rather be laid down
Where I can feel at home
Maybe I could be laid in town
Where I won't feel alone.

"Why not just put me in a place
Where I can hear a tune
Just lay me underneath the stage
In that Longhorn saloon."

Those were the last words that he said
They shrugged and said "Why not ?"
A cowboy in a bar who's dead
That ain't a brand new thought.

When you pass by in your new Fords
And wish to say a prayer
You'll find him undeneath them boards
The Longhorn S'loon's still there.

Longing for Kate
~~ Larry Bradfield – ©2012 ~~

I ain't seen it for myself, but
The boys all swore it's true.
There's a gal named Kate a ridin'
For the Bar S that's new.

Now that's just down the road apiece
As a curious man,
I'd mosey over, have a look,
And see as best I can.

Well I found her there a sittin'
On top a handsome bay.
Her long blonde hair was flowin' down
Her back in disarray.

To say that I was thunderstruck
Just surely said it well.
I'll dang sure take her out tonight
Or I'll be go to Hell !

I rode right up and spoke my mind,
Said I had lost my heart.
She said I'd better find it fast
Before them cows did part.

'Cause comin' through that bunch of beeves
Her jealous husband rode.
I looked at all his six foot six
And knew I'd hit the road.

I brooded o'er the loss that day
And couldn't rid my mind
Of things that might have come my way,
Of things I left behind.

The years passed by and then one day
I saw them in the store .
He don't look happy nowadays,
She weighs three hundred four.

That night I slept from dusk to dawn
My dreams were quiet at last.
No Kate was there to haunt me now
I can forget the past.

One Foot on the Porch
~~ Larry Bradfield – ©2012 ~~

He kept one foot in the stirrup
And one foot on her porch.
Wasn't sure what he was doin',
But he shore had the torch.

Didn't know just what he wanted,
Or just what he should say.
If she'd just give a little hint,
He knew he'd gladly stay.

But she was quiet, so was he,
Hoss was gettin' jumpy.
He had to move one of his feet,
'Fore he got plumb grumpy.

About that time a cat run by,
Was followed by a dog.
A bark and hiss, the hoss took off
And drug him like a log.

He bounced along about a block
Before his boot came loose.
He laid there in the dust awhile
And wondered "what's the use "?

She strolled right up to where he lay,
Said "Cowboy, you're a mess."
He gave a sheepish little grin
Said "That's what I would guess !"

She said "Just come along with me,
Dad's old clothes you'll borrow.
Just spend the night with me tonight,
Get the horse tomorrow."

She said "You've got to find a way
To say what's on your mind.
A better way than bein' dragged
I'm sure you're bound to find !"

The next time that they kissed goodnight
And he was homeward bound,
The hoss had noticed that his boss
Had both feet on the ground.

Winter Comes
~~ Larry Bradfield – ©2012 ~~

Where did you go while I stayed there
And Spring had come along
The world was ours a little while
I turned and you were gone

Now Winter's here, I still look back
The year is at its end
The world has turned its last for me
Where did you go, my friend

Don't Play Well With Others
~~ Larry Bradfield – ©2012 ~~

This new teachin' just ain't my style
It's way too deep for me
My boy's been learnin' for awhile
Some things I just can't see

A lot of things I'd just get rid
Like how we're all brothers
He wrote about Billy The Kid
"Don't play well with others"

His take on Jesse James is new
Somehow don't see the crime
He's got a different point of view
"A victim of his time"

Butch Cassidy and Sundance Kid
Seemed just like Robin Hood
No matter what they ever did
"Was for the greater good"

I found my boy out near the shed
Said "saddle up your roan.
Some things you've gotten in your head
Are better left alone."

We rode up to the timberline
Said "son, now look real good
No other place is near so fine
Nor deep within your blood.

Lewis and Clark passed over there,
Kit Carson rode right through
Dozens of hunters looked for bear
And trappers hunted too

The miners built the first real towns
And stayed the winters through
The cowboys grew in leaps and bounds
And gave us lots to do.

Now them folks that you're writin' of
Gave nothin' to this place
They only took with push and shove
And laughed in good folks' face

There ain't no way to make them good
They're killers through and through
Be proud of folks we know who would
Be just like me and you."

We rode back down to our homestead
That sheepish boy and I
He thinks of heroes now instead
Of psychos who passed by.

Modern Cowboys
~~ Larry Bradfied & Clark Crouch – ©2012 ~~

Cowboys today are rarely seen,
they don't ride herd no more,
'stead a ridin' Pinto ponies
they drive a four-by-four.

They've got their rifle racks in back
and cowhide on the seat,
they're wearin' huge new Stetson hats
and boots upon their feet.

These modern cowboys are not real,
them boots ain't seen no muck,
all they've ever seen of ranchin'
is from their pickup truck.

Horse Trainer
~~ Clark Crouch – ©2012 ~~

When Sam has broke a horse,
you've really gotta say
that Old Sam broke it well
in his own gentle way.

You might say it's well broke
and fit for western trails,
as gentle as can be,
'cause Old Sam never fails.

Except, of course, in town,
that's where he drops his pay,
drinkin', gamblin' and such,
'cause that is Old Sam's way.

So Sam is without cash,
he spent it havin' fun,
livin' high on the hog,
and now his spendin's done

There's just one thing to say,
which shouldn't be misspoke,
Old Sam's just like his horse
'cause both are really broke.

The Rancher and the Boy
~~ Clark Crouch – ©2013 ~~

The rancher lived an austere life,
and knew the gospel well
so he could speak with clarity
of heaven and of hell.

He spoke so much of brotherhood
and of the widow's mite,
the need to help your fellow man,
and do what e're is right.

Then one day he spotted a man,
unconscious 'side the road,
but turned his head away from that
as down the trail he rode.

But then a boy, a slender lad,
saw that same injured soul
and leaped right down from on his horse
determined to console.

He knew not how to help the man,
but comfort him he did
and raised him from a bed of thorns,
that slender youthful kid.

One spoke so well, though insincere,
the other leaped to aid
and did the things he felt were right
with no thought to evade.

Compare the rancher and the boy,
how each reacted there
to aid an injured fellow man
and give him needed care.

Words alone are insufficient
when someone suffers pain;
it takes a willingness to serve
and help him stand again.

Inland Sea
~~ Clark Crouch – ©2013 ~~

No ships sail this great inland sea,
no pirates are in view,
no captain mans the quarterdeck,
and there's no gallant crew.

No, this sea is not of water,
although it ebbs and flows
with great waves tossed by western winds,
waves rarely in repose.

It's wind-blown grasses making waves
to race across the hills
to splash, perhaps, on distant shores
to go where e'er it wills.

It's an ever-changing landscape
here in our western land…
grasses undulating, dancing,
in waves so far inland.

Cookie's Cuisine
~~ Clark Crouch – ©2013 ~~

There are biscuits in the oven
and supper's on the range;
it's a pot of Cookie's chili
with spices mighty strange.

It's got a-plenty beans and beef,
and chili powder too,
but what those other spices are
ain't got no place in stew.

Cookie's got no education,
his learnin' is quite slim,
and he learned his way of cookin'
in ways that suited him.

His coffee is like iodine,
his biscuits like boot heels
but it's the only food we've got
'though not the best of meals.

His spices may be willow bark
or Jimson weedy roots
and you'll have to take your chances,
'cause there'll be no disputes.

You're apt to get a belly ache
from eatin' Cookie's chuck
but you may actually survive
if you've a bit of luck.

But never ever do complain
'bout Cookie's fine cuisine
or else he will cook you somethin'
that really is obscene.

Advice to an Eight Year Old
~~ Clark Crouch – ©2013 ~~

When I was eight I had a dream;
a farrier I'd be
takin' care of all the horses,
that's just the life for me.

My hero was a farrier
and that became my aim,
to protect my father's horses
keep them from goin' lame.

But when I told my father that
he said, "you're just a lad
and if you don't quite reach that goal
don't let it make you sad."

"I wish you all the best in life,"
he said, with his lips pursed,
"but shoeing is a daunting task…
just learn to shoo flies first."

Duke Morrison
~~ *Clark Crouch* – ©*2013* ~~

I met the Duke in forty-eight…
he seemed a lonely guy,
sitting 'side the stage by himself
as others passed him by.

Although I'd never met the man,
I stopped to chat a while
and his lonely look disappeared,
his frown became a smile,

I learned a lot about that man
and of his work on screen
and, as he mentioned film titles,
most of them I'd seen,

It was a pleasure meeting Duke,
a kind and friendly man,
who talked at length with a young lad
who'd always be his fan.

'Though named Marion Morrison
before his western reign,
he became a western hero
known as the Duke, John Wayne.

The River Flowed
~~ *Neal Dachstadter – ©2013* ~~

From canyon cliff with cloudy sheen
Down gradient steep, severe and clean,
In draw, on bench, in tumbling stream,
Cold waters fell, with snow-melt green

To roots of Pine descending dank
Below the silted river bank,
With Aspen melding rank on rank,
The River flowed, and ever drank.

When men of gold descended, lank,
Then pans into the water sank,
Emerging bright, or merely blank
For humble shant or mansion swank

In busy towns along the flank,
Rich mercantiles with "clink" and "clank"
Mid prosperous echo "…Ma'am we thank"
The River flowed, and ever drank.

For roving Gambler (silken hank),
For weary Pioneer and Yank,
For Teacher, Parson, Doctor? Crank?
And Hickory stick, for boyhood prank,

Past screaming blade and sawmill plank,
Neath bell and steeple, water tank,
Mid frontier word, not minced but frank,
The River flowed, and ever drank.

Primeval birth or sands that sink,
Mid ancient day and future brink,
All time is present, e'er we think,
The River flows, and ever drinks.

Cold Winter, Wyoming
~~ Neal Dachstadter – ©2013 ~~

Yellowstone, Yellowstone, Kings to go forth
Yellowstone, Yellowstone, songs to the North
O Norther a-bluster, from left of the Dawn,
Proclaim the Cold Winter: "Come King and come Pawn,

Come Grizzly and Grouse, now Squirrel and Snake,
Fore the frost or the snow, mid a gold Aspen brake
Neath the shade of the Fir and the Pine and the Spruce
While the Buffalo graze with the Elk and the Moose."

Cherokee Gal
~~ Steve Dickson – ©2013 ~~

I met her on down at the county fair
She had a red dress on and a feather in her hair
So black and shiny like a raven's wing
My heart beatin' so fast but I couldn't do a thing

She smiled at me and she looked like the sun
Lightin' up the sky just as the daybreak has begun
I took her by the hand, gave her a twirl
As we danced all the night and I knew she was my girl

We ran with the wind, kissed under the moon
Time flew by so fast, our youth fled way too doggone soon
I'll always recall what I told my pal
I'm gonna go and marry that sweet Cherokee gal

The Race at the Old County Fair
~~Steve Dickson – ©2013 ~~

Horses came from near and far
On that fine and sunny day
Rich and poor men brought 'em out
On that afternoon in May

Paints and Arabs, Appys too
Many other breeds were there
Racin' for the braggin' rights
At the local county fair

Banker brought his thoroughbred
They all said that horse was fast
Ran him at the Derby once
But he came in next to last

One feller brought a donkey
Another rode on a mule
They were banned from the big race
So they had a private duel

Nine horses stood at the line
But then just before the shot
Feller ran up out of breath
Said 'look here what I done brought'

He opened up his trailer
Rode on over to the rest
On a ugly swayback beast
The line judge said sir you jest

The horse looked just plumb awful
Had a humpy roman nose
One ear was gone completely
And a rank aroma rose

He walked up to the others
They sure didn't want him there
Fussin' and a fidgetin'
With noses up in the air

The shot rang out, they were gone
A runnin' down the dirt track
The thoroughbred was leadin'
the rest of the motley pack

The race was going his way
Then the crowd was filled with ire
As the plug was gainin' ground
Runnin' like his butt's afire

History was made that day
Many lost a lot of cash
Most bet on the thoroughbred
He sure didn't win that dash

No other horse was faster
When once they got him started
Nine horses would not beat him
None could outrun Hoof Hearted

My Little Town
~~ Steve Dickson – ©2013 ~~

I left town at seventeen
Went far away to war
Never made it back this way
My family was no more

Parents died while I was gone
None left to run the farm
I stayed on in the service
So none would come to harm

I married and had children
Kids asked where I was from
we drove in just yesterday
To see what has become

Main street was plumb deserted
The shops were all shut down
I drove on to the feed store
Out at the edge of town

Hollis was at the counter
He'd been a friend to dad
His big old hands were shaking
His face looked tired and sad

He told us all the story
Of what had come to pass
In this town not long ago
Out on the prairie grass

"Folks were forced to sell their land
When big boys moved on in
They're growin crops unheard of
I tell ya it's a sin

Usin' all them chemicals
Folks was gettin' real sick
Killed off lots of their livestock
It's just a mean ol' trick

They want to do this frackin'
Promise life much higher
Others say it's no darn good
Claim water lights on fire

I've been here all my life, boy
This town gave me a start
People had small businesses
Replaced by a Walmart

Our little town is hurtin'
Won't ever be the same
All across America
And greed is what's to blame

Buffalo Moon
~~ Steve Dickson – ©2013 ~~

They danced by the pale moonlight
Called to spirits of the past
To bring the herds back to them
Thus ending harsh winter's fast

Thunder runs on the prairie
As they top the furthest rise
So vast in countless numbers
Woolly treasure for dark eyes

Taking just what was needed
No such thing to them as waste
Gave thanks to the Creator
Simple life not ruled by haste

Every year they came back strong
'Til the time when great beasts fell
When strangers came in shooting
Left a rotting stinking hell

Foolish men just took the hides
Left the carcass in the sun
People gazed in agony
At the evil that was done

Gone now from golden prairies
So few ever to return
Slaughtered and forgotten now
No good lesson did men learn

I saw an old man crying
Once not very long ago
As he remembered seeing
All those bodies in the snow

Ghosts and bones are scattered now
In the places once called home
Rare now are the buffalo
Where vast millions once did roam

Dakota Wind
~~ Steve Dickson – ©2013 ~~

Wind blows cold on the prairie now
Where the people used to roam
Living close with nature's spirit
Many places were called home

Herds of buffalo shared the land
The great bounty of the earth
Was theirs as far as eye could see
They knew how much it was worth

Far more than any golden dust
Torn and stolen from black hills
The strange ones came from far and wide
Brought with them so many ills

Old clan members just wanted peace
The younger men talked of war
Many were sickened by disease
Their numbers fell by the score

Forced to sign away all their past
They were driven from the land
Sent far away against their will
By a cruel misguided hand

A mournful wind on the prairie
Blows hard on their run down shacks
The people chase different spirits
Poverty follows their tracks

Can hope rise up from the ashes
To replace what's now despair
If the young learn that the old ones
Can inspire and make them care

Return again to nature's path
Even in these modern days
Let go now of the tragic past
Live once more in ancient ways

Half Moon Pass
~~ Steve Dickson — ©2013 ~~

We left at dawn with stock all packed
To hunt for elk and deer
Way up high near the Half Moon Pass
Where mountain streams run clear

The sun was bright and it was warm
when we rode from the ranch
Stayed that way 'til we took the fork
Up where the rivers branch

We made our camp and settled in
Built us a little fire
Smell of the woods was mighty fine
As the moon rose higher

We told tales of days long gone by
Some might have been white lies
Me and Bill, just two good old friends
Under the western skies

The next day we went way up high
To a green meadow where
Sweet grass grows that draws in the herds
That come to feed up there

We stopped and left the horses tied
Right near the heavy brush
We crept up on our hands and knees
So quiet in no rush

Saw ten big muleys grazin' there
A big bull elk as well
As we stood up and raised our guns
Behind us on came hell

I heard my pack mule brayin' loud
Things happened all too fast
Big grizzly hammered Bill's old horse
She fell and breathed her last

The grizz stood up and looked at us
He was near ten foot tall
Must have run a good half a ton
We could not run at all

He must have been a trailin' us
We'd surely seen no signs
Of this mean and fearsome critter
Whilst ridin' through the pines

He came full bore at both of us
Seemed moments stood stock still
I took a shot but missed the mark
He came in for the kill

He knocked me down and chawed my head
I grabbed hold of my knife
Stuck it hard in his stinkin' neck
Mad fighting for my life

He tore off all of my left ear
But I still heard the blast
Of Bill's old fifty caliber
As hot lead whistled past

It took the bear some time to die
As I was layin' there
Starin' at the Montana sky
And wishin' you were there

Bill patched me up and got me out
To him I owe my life
The ride back home down that mountain
Was filled with pain and strife

We still go on hunts together
At this same time each year
Sometimes I find my eyes aground
Lookin' for that darned ear.

A Friend at the End of the Line
~~ Steve Dickson – ©2013 ~~

I rode in here from months on the trail
to this small town west of the divide
Days were long and I sure did not fail
The big herd sold and few critters died

Been alone now for most of my days
Since my children and bride passed away
The sharp pain in my heart has its ways
Of keeping most all others at bay

Still I yearn for a gal at my side
To share livin' and laughter and fun
Bein' free and so open and wide
But I've hidden my soul from the sun

I see a girl stand there in the glow
With the summer's warm wind in her hair
I'd give most anything just to know
That for this here ol' cowboy she'd care

I ride on over to her and say
"Could I visit for a spell with you
I'm alone in this ol' world today
And just feelin' a little bit blue"

"Why sir, yes please get off'n your horse
I'd be gladdened to spend time with you
Now, forgive me for being so coarse
But it might cost a dollar or two"

"Ma'am my old heart would likely plumb bust
If we dallied in that kind of way
My hot blood is filled mostly with rust
And intentions ain't leanin' toward play"

So we spent near the whole afternoon
When I left town I felt mighty fine
We shared stories, she sang me a tune
While she hung out her wash on the line

The Bronc Rider
~~ Steve Dickson – ©2012 ~~

He was sittin' at the Palace Bar there on Whiskey Row
Done takin' on his part here in the oldest rodeo
Busted up and sore and tired, thoughts stirring in his hard head
Thinkin' of them jumps he took that make him now want a bed

The pickup men surely saved his ass once or twice at least
That last big painted stallion was a strong and mean ol' beast
He rode ever' hoss they gave him, and man it was a chore
Gettin' hard to jump back up and then make eight seconds more

His legs were bowed from many days lived out there on the range
When too much time was spent indoors it made him feel so strange
Some rough stock that he rode today near 'bout just done him in
But he sure cowboyed up my friend and then he took the win

As he's nursin' a cold bottle and ponderin' the past
Some tourist folks come walkin' in and stop and stand aghast
At the sight of this here fella all dusty and threadbare
Wearin' chaps and faded jeans with straw and dirt in his hair

One ol' gal she sauntered on up and said "excuse me sir
It looks like you were in a wreck" he slowly turned to her
"Now Ma'am I beg your pardon if I look so rough to you
But you're likely not to understand what it is I do

I ride broncos for a livin' and they don't want me there
They run and jump and try their best to toss me in the air
Some are unsuccessful but most others have their own way
I'll end up down there on my butt in dirt and crap and hay

My back is sore and my durn neck is mendin' from last week
I landed on my noggin' and for a while could not speak
I've busted nearly all the bones that docs have ever named
Been throwed from wolves that surely will forever be untamed

"Why ride those mean wild horses if it makes you hurt so bad?"
"Lady all I'm knowin' is in the saddle I am glad
Throughout the week I work the herds a roamin' far and wide
When Friday comes I head on out to take a rougher ride

I know it may seem loco and just a little funny
To earn so many broken bones for so little money"
But you know I'd do it though if it didn't pay a lick
Cuz ridin' on them mean wild horses is what makes me tick

We do our jobs together and put on a darned good show
Both knowin' we will work so hard a goin' toe to toe
Travelin' the circuit is now the only life I know
When my wallet's near 'bout empty, I'm off to rodeo

So please pardon my appearance and dusty presence here
But this 'ol town made history on the wild west frontier
Where all the roughest cowboys travel far to show their stuff
At the world's oldest rodeo and competition's tough

Now go on out and see the sights in this big western land
Where sky is blue and folks are few and sunsets are so grand
Take time to learn the history not so long in the past
If you spend time with ranchin' folks, you'll understand at last

Raja and His Chuckwagon Days
~~ Steve Dickson – ©2012 ~~

He looked real funny dressed up in them duds
when we come in to camp from the trail
Washin' tin plates in a tubful o' suds
Shiny derby hat hung on a nail

Who's this little feller we want to know
a dandy here among us old dogs
He's the new cookie, said the trail boss, Joe
as we set down on one of the logs

The old cook had died 'bout three weeks ago
We'd been livin' just mostly on beans
hell on our innards I want you to know
we near blew out the seats of our jeans

Shorty brought biscuits and set em on down
Then next up came some fine smellin' stew
we looked real close as he come back around
and poured us all some hot coffee too

Nary a word he said nothin' at all
'Til Bob asked where the hell he was from
"I come from a village 'round old Cornwall"
we all stared at him like we was dumb

"My name is Raja and I'll be your man
Cooking fine fare daily for you gents
Now bring me your dishes and fetch those pans
So I can earn all my meager pence

We started laughin' and near 'bout fell down
This first time we heard Raja talkin'
Feller looked jus' like a little ol' clown
Voice sounded like he was a squawkin'

The other bunch come in and asked around
"Is that the new cookie that Joe hired?"
Said Bob who was pettin' his 'ol red hound
"If he cain't cook he'll surely be fired."

Joe said "give the rascal a fightin' chance
Townfolks said he's the best in the bunch
He ain't much to look at on the first glance
But he'll surely be cookin' your lunch

We teased him, no mercy for several days
Though his cookin' sure tasted real swell
We found great amusement at his strange ways
Until he rang that 'ol dinner bell

Raja was picky when it came to meals
most game that we brought to him, he'd snub
While serving he'd stand and dig in his heels
He got mad if we called his food grub

He wouldn't join us when we went to town
He stayed by the chuckwagon all day
Kept to himself but if some were around
He'd pull out his fiddle and he'd play

Had a fine voice and he knew some sweet tunes
That caused us hard 'ol cowboys to cry
He sang in a language from ancient runes
That were written in days long gone by

One day Jim poured gin in his cup of tea
Raja coughed and sputtered all that day
When supper was over he came to me
This here's what all he managed to say

"You fellows have had enough of your fun
I allowed you chaps to have your play
Go choose now amongst you the roughest one
I'll knock his bloody block off, I say"

"Doggone it Raja, you're too small to fight
Most of these 'ol boys are jus' plum mean
They'd stomp and whup you and turn out your light
I'm thinkin' you're jus' a bit too green"

He stared there at me with sparks in his eye
Said "I challenge your best man right now
Wager your eagles and I'll show you why
And in a few moments you'll see how

He puffed up like a rooster dancin' 'round
He was swingin but no one was there
We stood in wonder but looked at the ground
Old Jubal said "Hell, I'll take the dare"

Now Jubal's a big un o'er six foot tall
He claimed to have wrassled with a bear
He never laid hand on Raja at all
Brother, what we seen there was plum rare

Jubal went to swing but took a big lick
Seems like Raja struck twenty more blows
Our man was wheezin,' just tryin' to kick
How Jubal kept a standin', Lord knows

He finally fell over out like a light
Little Raja was still fit and fresh
You wouldn't know he'd just been in a fight
There weren't a doggone mark on his flesh

We picked up Jubal, his bell was still rung
Said his noggin was filled with a buzz
For two hours after his head was hung
Until Raja explained who he was

He gathered us 'round down there at the camp
His bright curly red hair stickin' up
"Good fellows I tell you that I'm the champ
Of all England and still hold the Cup

I've been a boxer for most of me life
I learned the fine skill when just a lad
I was married but had a jealous wife
I fled when she caught me being bad

Here to the states then I made me own way
Learned culinary art at fine schools
I swore not to box unless 'twas for pay
Me hands can also be deadly tools

Honest me hearties, I'm now on the lam
From me missus and me former foes
If they find me gents, life's not worth a damn
Time on earth here would be full of woes

He fixed a platter of pork chops and kale
With potaters and biscuits and tea
We swore his secret was safe and this tale
Brother you didn't hear it from me

The Bullfighter
~~ *Steve Dickson – ©2012* ~~

In days gone past they called you a clown
But there's nothin' fun when a bull runs you down
A ton of mad beef throwin' a fit
You have to jump in there to take on the hit

Some think eight seconds goes by real quick
Son, it's a long time for a cowboy to stick
Most men don't make it for the whole ride
The good ones bear down and just take it in stride

Climb in the chute and pray you'll be there
When that rank bull throws 'em up high in the air
Buckin', jumpin' and twistin' around
That mean ol' critter wants 'em down on the ground

So's he can stomp and stick 'em and gore
Until they can't get up at all any more
You're in the middle of that big storm
When both man and beast are in rare fightin' form

You have to lay your life on the line
To help those young men and make sure they are fine
When the dust settles at the day's end
The bull riders all know that you're their best friend

River of No Return
~~ Steve Dickson – ©2012 ~~

South of Stanley Idaho
This river starts its run
From high up in the mountains
Near Valley of the Sun

A little trickle wandrin'
Winds through the fertile land
A subtle hint of magic
She's not yet showed her hand

Soon you'll come to Redfish Lake
Make camp and stay a spell
Far down in the waters deep
There's many tales to tell

The swift young stream is flowing
Wind whispers in tall trees
In mist of early morning
Watch ospreys ride the breeze

The basin holds the ranches
That make this country great
Livestock and game graze grasses
That grow so tall and straight

Ride into the wilderness
The Sawtooth mountains rise
Lost River goes underground
Far south is her surprise

Take Middle Fork, test your luck
Where fast white water flows
You may see a muley buck
As he courts his brown eyed does

Through canyons come a roaring
Wild music to your ears
Drink deep of sweet clear nectar
Long running all these years

Chinook lay in quiet pools
Beside a fallen tree
Make their way to spawning grounds
Come far from deep blue sea

Hardy folks have come and gone
They searched long for bright gold
Looking for that special place
Their secrets seldom told

Glide between the soaring cliffs
Where ancient spirits dwell
Taking naught but memories
Tales you will always tell

This living stream is a gem
For all my days I'll yearn
to spend time on this wondrous
River of No Return

Country Woman
~~ Steve Dickson – ©2012 ~~

She handles the big old wagon
When we bring in the hay
She feeds the stock and rides and ropes
She works so hard all day

With no crying or complaining
At bills we have to pay
I can't bring her fancy diamonds
Or take her far away

But I sure do take her dancing
And we know how to play
As we walk our fertile meadows
And give thanks every day

You know all the golden riches
Just surely can't compare
To the sight of my sweet lady
When she takes down her hair

She is all my joy and comfort
My partner and my life
I'm so proud to stand beside her
To know she is my wife.

Big Hat
~~ Steve Dickson – ©2011 ~~

One fine summer day so long ago
I had made big plans but didn't know
of the gift a man would soon bestow
That shaped my life and helped me to grow

The Old Spring Creek was flowing so clear
Those big rainbow trout were always near
The cottonwoods were just raining down
White magic clouds land soft on the ground
In my own small Montana home town

Beneath the bridge I would cast my bait
I never did have too long to wait
To bring in my limit day by day
I learned how to fish most every way

That Saturday folks filled up the town
So many came in from all around
There was to be a great wild west show
And this wasn't just a rodeo

I spent that morning down at the creek
And later me and my pals would sneak
Up on the fence down at the corrals
To watch the cowboys and painted gals

While I was just packin' up my gear
A horse drawn wagon was drawin' near
As it passed by up above my head
There was a holler, a cuss word said
That turned my jug ears a shade of red

Then from the sky a dark shadow fell
Whatever it was I could not tell
It landed so softly at my feet
And caused my young heart to skip a beat

A big old hat with a feathered band
I never saw nothing quite so grand
Stetson branded with a beaver blend
Straight from cowboy heaven God did send
Delivered unto my smelly hand

I put it on just like a gold crown
And all it did was just fall right down
I couldn't see, and felt like a clown
As I tumbled to the mossy ground

I wore it down to the wild west show
Stuffed with newspaper so none would know
That it weren't mine, I would never tell
Yet I still feared goin' straight to hell

A hatless young cowboy rode that day
He rode everything that came his way
Then he walked to me and had a frown
I nearly turned my 'ol britches brown

He took that Stetson from my bald head
Then put it right back on there instead
He grinned wide at me and then he said
'Now boy, I surely do like that hat
I had me one just the same as that
Now you make sure that it don't get lost
Or get too tore up when you get tossed'

I wore it so proudly come what may
Later I too gave that hat away
For I learned a lesson on that day
Which inside my heart will always stay

A cowboy's much more than just a hand
He surely knows how to take a stand
To do that what's right and what is good
This old way of life is understood

Dancin' In The Dust
~~ *Steve Dickson – ©2012* ~~

That darn ol' brindle bull made me chase him for three whole days
I was bound to sell him off for his mean and ornery ways
He rattled up the cowboys and tore down most of the fence
I would have shot the rascal but his head was just too dense

My horse was in cahoots with him, and wouldn't push him hard
I had him near the barn one time, he went right through the yard
The wife was hangin' out the wash, he took the clothesline down
Then ran off with her bloomers stuck there on his horny crown

He headed for the river and I followed close behind
Them drawers just made him madder as they caused him to be blind
He ran right down in the water and then just stood stock still
I lit down from off the saddle and got real close until

He turned and then the undies fell, I had no place to go
I tossed the lasso true and well, a real dandy throw
It caught him low around them horns and then the fight was on
He pulled me across the river and he was almost gone

I dug in my old Noconas, tied off around a stump
He nearly pulled it from the ground but didn't get the jump
I got two other ropes on him but not enough to trust
Rightly so for next I know we was dancin' in the dust

That bull bucked and kicked and bellered and put on one wild show
I hopped and ducked and did my best but little did I know
The herd of cows had gathered round, I guess to watch the fun
A young heifer chewed the ropes in two, off with them he run

Never in my wranglin' days had I seen me such a sight
Or tangled with a durn critter that put up such a fight
Now on our ranch it's peaceful, I never did sell that bull
Them heifers keep him busy and his dance card's always full

The Old Timer
~~ Steve Dickson – ©2010 ~~

He's coming through the passes
Across the great Divide
Through seas of golden grasses
On this, his final ride

He's been with us for ages
A writer of the past
Been through most of the stages
Which our short lives are cast

He's sailed across the oceans
Fought hard in all the wars
Not one to show emotions
He opened up the doors

A cowboy or a teacher
A tailor or a cook
A soldier or a preacher
Whatever else it took

To make our country greater
We all owe him our thanks
It must be soon, not later
God's thinning out his ranks

I'm glad I got to know him
To see all of his sides
As evening light now grows dim
I stop, and on he rides

Trails End
~~ Steve Dickson – ©2009 ~~

I'm riding to the setting sun
With none to call my friend
Save for my faithful, gentle horse
And we are near the end

We've covered many miles today
And left our dusty track
Upon this here old mother earth
How could we pay her back

For giving us so many days
And evenings by the fire
She shared with us her sacred ways
It's time now to retire

The path now seems to fall away
From solid ground below
We lift our eyes up to the clouds
Much higher still we'll go

Our time it seems has run it's course
The sun is sinking low
Pass on the word that we are near
Let's start this rodeo

Moonlight in Montana
~~ Steve Dickson – ©2012 ~~

I was a young bull rider
She was a rodeo queen
We made the rounds together
There was much we had not seen

She rode a barrel racer
I stayed on the rankest bull
From town to town we traveled
Summer days were always full

I never had the courage
To take her soft hand in mine
Until one moonlit evening
In Montana in the pines

I told her that I loved her
while we stood there in the night
From then we were not parted
Long sweet nights by firelight

We built a home together
Worked our days hard side by side
Life was good, it was our time
But it ended with that ride

A cold day in September
Brought her young life to an end
The horse slipped and fell on her
I said goodbye to my friend

She's up there in those mountains
I spend much time with her there
The moonlight in Montana
Still so hard for me to bear

Tom Horn
~~ Steve Dickson – ©2012 ~~

To ride the range all day
Running cattle did not pay
You searched more for a thrill
Then you found it in the kill

Scouted for Uncle Sam
Sought those who were on the lam
Apache tongue you know
Helped take down Geronimo

Pinkertons hired you then
Paid you well to hunt for men
You seemed to lust for blood
It came later in a flood

You done it all old son
Made a living by the gun
Chased outlaws on the trail
Tracked hard men and did not fail

Wyoming was your home
Far from there you did not roam
Big ranchers ruled the land
Foreign money in their hand

Homesteaders came to stay
Free land called those far away
Land barons paid your bills
You shot settlers from the hills

You warned them to clear out
If they stayed there was no doubt
That soon they would be dead
From ambush filled with hot lead

Winchester '94
Did your dirty work and more
They say you had no heart
Was it that way from the start?

Then came that fateful day
A lad shot from far away
The best shot that you made
And for that your life was paid
>
A marshal lured you in
He then filled you full of gin
You bragged about the way
The Nickell boy died that day

They hung you out to dry
Ranchers would not testify
The jury was not moved
Though your guilt could not be proved

The locals were dismayed
An example must be made
The old ways would not stand
1900 was at hand

You hung there in '03
From a gallows not a tree
You calmly met your fate
As Julian made you wait

Your story's been retold
Of a man who broke the mold
Of an outlaw out for pay
Or a good man gone astray

We all know in the end
There are laws we should not bend
The Lord don't hold a grudge
Only He could be your judge

The Circuit Preacher
~~ *Stephen Foster – ©2012* ~~

He rode soaking wet with water
And he chilled nearly to the bone
Along the slippery flooded path
The man of God traveled alone,

What drives a man beyond himself
To travel in the worse weather
To journey forth atop his mule
His only friend saddle leather,

Can the Word mean so much to him
He would follow a wagon track
Just to reclaim one wayward soul
Traveling the hidden trail and back

On a three hundred mile circuit
Aboard a temperamental mule
Led on by his trust in the Lord
There were many thought him a fool,

On an old mule that was spavined
Oft tied upright in the saddle
Through flood crested river and swamp
Called by the Lord to do battle,

He preached in the small rustic chapels
Beneath a canopy of trees
He preached to the great town sized crowds
And to small groups of twos and threes,

Earning fifteen dollars a year
Just don't seem like it was worth it
But the man on that tired old mule
Loved the Lord and just wouldn't quit,

Celebrating the newly born
Grieving the dearly departed
A minister to all their needs
The joyful and broken hearted,

The Circuit Preacher had traveled
Where so many had shunned the road
Going to the most distant places
To see the seeds of God were sowed.

Where the Green Grass Grows
~~ *Stephen Foster – ©2014* ~~

Silent now the battlefield
The angry sword is sheathed,
No sign of the destruction
Or cannon, gun smoke wreathed.

The battle scared now gone
Back home to the ones they love,
On the field the sign of peace
Seen in the flight of a dove.

Cannon set in perfect rows
A remembrance of the past,
Each one of them is now spiked
The final shot was their last.

A soldier of stone stands now
His rifle at the ready,
Monument of those who stood
Troops both faithful and steady.

They are here still those who fell
Now aligned in perfect rows,
They lie beneath the markers
Silent where the green grass grows.

Where the green grass grows they fought
The cause now doesn't matter,
Think of all the families
The lives these deaths would shatter.

My thought then turns to prayer
Beside every soldier's grave,
Remember the sacrifice
Precious life they freely gave.

My Forest Camp
~~ *Stephen Foster – ©2014* ~~

Cricket chirps a serenade,
A silent pond comes alive.
Voices of a hundred frogs,
Orchestra begins to thrive.

The night bird's sound in concert
In shrill tones his voice blending,
Barn owl with a sometimes hoot
Deep base moan is it sending.

And to hear a distant crack,
A dead branch in submission,
Winds weight to no longer bear
Adds to this nights tradition.

Moonlight shinning through canvas,
Dance of ethereal shade,
Lying upon the firm ground
In this bed that I have made.

In peace on the restful edge,
That time when sleep's blanket falls
With the sounds of night fading,
Mind closing to evening calls.

I drift to a different plain,
In truth only a spirit,
Approach that heavenly place
To embrace, not to fear it.

Thankful for this restful scene,
Heavenly peace, my delight,
Then drawn from peaceful musings
By the breaking of dawns light.

Wakened in my forest camp,
Thankful for all things living,
In awe of our mighty God
And this life of His giving.

What Would the Lone Ranger Think
~~ *Stephen Foster – ©2014* ~~

I grew up with western heroes
They were our daily family fare,
There was no doubt of good or bad
The hero always seemed to care.

So it gives me cause to wonder
Just what would the Lone Ranger think,
The helpless maiden bared it all,
Met him at the door with a drink.

Tonto scalped the desperado,
He made an awful bloody mess.
Chester fired a branding iron,
Marshall Dillon made him confess.

You just can't watch television,
It seems that lately more and more
Every time you turn on the tube
There is a fest of sex and gore.

To know they had been abandoned,
All the good things we had been taught,
The old Ranger would just be hurt,
His values are no longer sought.

Oh for the days of yesteryear
When the Lone Ranger rode the plain,
Riding with his good friend Tonto
To bring only good, never pain.

Southwestern Sky
~~ Delia J. Fry – ©2013 ~~

Colors of the Southwest sunset
Peeking through the shadows
A beautiful pastel palette
As the Southwest wind blows

Riders are anxious to get home
Images in the haze
Tracking through the muddy, clay loam
Blinking at the sun's rays

How many miles have they traveled
And how many sunsets
And all the paths that were brambled
Sleeping on worn blankets

Riders slowly inching their way
Windy days and cold nights
Wanting to camp and end the day
'Neath stars, Southwestern lights

Ghosts in the Mist
~~ Del Gustafson – ©2013 ~~

We had some rain fall yesterday but it was hot today,
The heat and humidity was unusual for late May,
We were gathering up our cattle in the foothills to the east,
And the weather in the mountains wasn't fit for man nor beast.

We suffered through that muggy heat until the day was done,
Then started down the mountain riding toward the setting sun,
Dusk was falling quickly, the sun dipped behind a hill,
Air that was hot and humid was now taking on a chill.

The ground fog was rising and through the thin blue haze,
I saw some rangy cattle that had filed out to graze.
Long horns adorned their polls, their bodies built for speed,
different in so many ways from the Herford cows we breed.

They raised their heads, keeping watch but didn't run in fear,
Silently moving as I rode close, much like a herd of deer,
I shook out a loop to rope one but as I rolled it with my wrist,
They glided off and disappeared like ghosts into the mist.

Cow Docs
~ *Del Gustafson ©2013* ~

The day is hot the dust is deep,
the calves are all well grown,
Big. strong and range bred wild,
it's hard to get them thrown.

Wild eyed at the ropes end,
Bucking and bawling in fright,
Until one snorts and shakes his head,
And then goes on the fight.

Tail raised, he drops his head,
Charging right at the crew,
The cowboys running for the fence,
As the steer comes busting through.

A cowboy tangled in the rope,
Had better try to get unwound.
Before the steer charges off,
Dragging him across the ground.

If a cowboy can't beat him to the fence?
The one thing that you can trust,
The Steer will knock that cowboy flat.
And roll him in the dust.

Rope burns, bruises, busted ribs,
Painful stomped on feet,
The cowboys may need more doctoring,
Then the stock they meant to treat.

Dust
~~ *Del Gustafson ©2013* ~~

I cough and wheeze, gasp and then sneeze,
From the cloud blown by the last gust.
Slapping a rope to the rear of a slow moving steer,
As we move in that billowing dust.

Dust from my hat to boot toes, dust up my nose,
A powder the color of rust.
Those thin boney steers from their tails to their ears,
Look alike in their coating of Dust.

The wind blows it around till it falls to the ground,
Where it settles to a hard barren crust,
We need rain I know to make the grass grow,
But all we get is more dust.

We couldn't plant cotton or grain for lack of rain,
Another year and I think I'll go bust.
We sold the tractors and plows to buy feed for the cows,
They couldn't survive on just dust.

My loan payments are due and my taxes are too,
And I feel it is really unjust,
What we produce on this land has no demand,
There just is no market for dust.

The Preacher said friend it will come to an end,
Stay strong in your faith and your trust,
But I'm afraid when I die it will still be bone dry,
And I'll return as just more blowing dust.

Honest Herb
~ *Del Gustafson ©2013* ~

I met up with Herb the other day as he came riding down the trail,
He had a young pinto mustang tied to his horse's tail,
I gave her a good look over, Herb never said a word,
But I suspected he had roped her from a mountain mustang herd.

I said, Herb, the thing about your horse chasing I never understood,
You go to church most Sundays and folks say you are good,
But I'm thinking about that Paint filly tied to your horse's tail,
If the BLM caught you with her you'd be fined or go to jail.

I know you think the government is run by crooks and fools,
We caught horses there for years before they changed the rules,
They round them up and ship them off, they spoiled all our fun,
But they will arrest a man for stealing if they catch him taking one.

Herb replied, you know I am a Deacon and that my faith is strong,
And I have always been a true friend and will never do you wrong,
Another man's cash or a branded calf, you know I'd never take it,
And any law that I agree with, there's no way I'd ever break it.

But the property tax and grazing fees are really getting high,
And with feed and groceries going up we are barely getting by,
And federal and state income tax on every dime I earn,
So I try to catch a horse or two as a little tax return.

I looked that filly over and scratched my head in thought,
She sure had better breeding than the last horse that I bought,
The government might call it stealing and claim that it is wrong,
But next time Herb goes chasing mustangs, I'm gonna tag along.

Cattle Drive
~ Del Gustafson ©2013 ~

It was Reconstruction Texas and everyone was poor,
We hadn't seen no money for a couple years or more,
But there were lots of cows in Texas worth money we were told,
If we could get them up to Kansas to trade for Yankee gold.

We decided to put the word out we were looking for some hands,
To gather up some cattle that weren't wearing brands,
We spread the word around the county, telling everyone,
We were needing willing cowboys, bring your saddle and a gun.

Some were old confederate soldiers, but most of them were young,
Two were hard case outlaws, afraid they'd be caught and hung,
We drove the wild cows we found out of the brushy breaks,
Some of the ones that carried brands the cook turned into steaks.

We found a place to pen them, up a canyon near the red,
We kept chasing cows through the brush till we had a thousand head,
There were a bunch more branded cows we decided to take along,
And hoped no one noticed because we knew that it was wrong.

We gathered a remuda, around eighty head or so
Most of them were borrowed but the owners didn't know,
Caught with stolen horses, there would be no judge and jury,
So we herded up that bunch of cows and moved them in a hurry,

We tried to keep them moving till we were deep in Indian lands,
The Red was running low so we lost no cows or hands.
Warriors watched us from their ponies as we moved across their grass,
We'd cut them out a cow or two and they always let us pass.

It seemed to take forever to cross that Kansas plain,
The men were ready for a town, most had never seen a train,
Months of heat and blowing dust getting our cattle to the rail,
Then heard that Texas Rangers had been following our trail,

After the long trail from Texas, we were ready to cut loose,
but found that we were wanted, maybe staring at a noose,
We decided not to bathe or shave, just find a cattle buyer,
Before we were recognized from that Texas wanted flyer.

When the buyer made an offer, he didn't have to offer twice,
We just stood and nodded when he threw out his first price,
We just took his money and then we galloped out of town,
If the Rangers caught up with us, they would probably gun us down.

Those two hard case cowboys, Waco and Captain Black,
Said, We've had enough of running so now we're heading back.
We served with Hood's Texas Brigade throughout this past War.
We are still free born Texans and we're not retreating anymore.

I heard they found those Texas Rangers who were following our track,
With Sixguns blazing, Rebel Yells they launched their last attack,
Their charge carried them through that bunch, they made to the rear,
Then whirled their mounts and charged again, selling their lives dear.

Those that went back to Texas for their mothers or their wives,
I heard the rangers caught them and those cowboys lost their lives,
The Rangers caught them one by one, ignoring their family's plea,
Tore them from their loved ones arms and hanged them from a tree.

I meant to avoid the hangman's noose or years in a Texas jail,
I rode north on a big fast horse till I cut the Oregon trail,
If I'd gone back to Texas I'd have ended like the rest,
So when I found that rutted trail I turned my good horse west.

I followed the trail to Oregon and drifted all around,
I was far enough from Texas so I'd be never found,
The day came when I decided It was time to kick off my boots,
And this high Oregon desert was the place to put down roots

I filed on a nice piece of land, cut by a good creek branch,
I built a cabin and holding pens, the beginnings of my ranch.
Summer heat and winter cold, made those years a battle.
Catching and breaking mustangs and trading them for cattle

I have settled into this new life, I've really changed my ways.
The years have passed and I can scarce recall my wild Texas days,
My land and herds have prospered, I am a big rancher now,
Still I wouldn't lynch a cowboy for rustling a cow.

My thoughts return from time to time to that cattle drive,
Memories of good friends lost will often come alive,
If I returned to Texas with a hundred hired guns,
Could I hunt down those Rangers and hang the guilty ones?

The Stranger
~ Del Gustafson ©2013 ~

He rode up to the cabin,
The air was cold and still,
His ragged Mackinaw was old,
And did not keep out the chill.

The barn collapsed years ago,
A pile without form,
He blanketed his horse with his slicker,
Trying to keep him warm.

His ride had been bitter cold,
As through the drifts he strove,
He had coal oil for the oil lamps,
And wood to feed the stove.

He had not crossed this threshold,
In fifty years or more,
He felt a wave of deep remorse,
As he stepped through the door.

He laid a fire in the stove,
And got it burning bright,
Filled the lamps and trimmed the wicks,
To fill the room with light.

He brewed a pot of coffee,
In Ma's enamelware pot,
And spread a simple Christmas meal,
From the few things he had brought.

As he sat and sipped his coffee,
In his mind he could still see,
The meals his mother served there,
The decorations on the tree.

This cabin he had once called home,
A refuge filled with joy,
With Ma and Pa and sisters,
He was the only boy.

He wiped the family pictures,
That were still hanging there,
And took his seat near the stove,
In the remains of Pa's old chair.

This home was once filled with love,
Joy and Christmas trees,
The crackling fire made him recall,
Those long gone memories.

The sound of Pa's loud laughter,
Ma's giggles and her smile,
Soft whispers of his sisters,
Lived again for a short while.

He'd ridden out on his own trail,
And the years had rolled on past,
His loved ones now were dead and gone,
He was the very last.

This will be his last ride,
His pilgrimage now was done,
He'll ride out, not to return,
With the rising of the sun.

Wild Herds
~~ Del Gustafson ©2013 ~~

The prairie stretches far as can be seen,
Under a deep blue sky
Cloud chimneys ride the upper winds,
Giant white pillars drifting by.

The golden grass heads bow as one,
Bent by the constant breeze.
Prairie flowers with purple blooms,
Rise above my horse's knees.

The cattle move slow in the summer heat,
With head and horns hanging low.
They want to lie down to chew their cud,
And with reluctance plod on slow.

Then distantly the drumming of hooves,
Faint at first but very clear,
The hoof beats grow louder still,
galloping, galloping, coming near.

Wild horses stream over the grassy plain,
Breathtakingly beautiful in their flight,
All colors of duns, sorrels, bays and roans
Piebald steeds of brown and white.

The magnificent herd passed and disappeared,
Running, running, on and on.
The prairie surrendered to the farmers plow,
And the wild herds were gone.

Dance With Me, Mister
~~ Lynn Kopelke — ©2013 ~~

Hey, mister, hey are you all right?
That was sure a bad one
Looked like you might take flight
You'd have thought the ground was a girl
The way you up and kissed her
Yeah, you're all right. C'mon
Dance with me Mister

I'll be your friend
I know it don't seem like that now
Me being all snorty and bucking so hard
But show me a little know how, grit and patience
And you'll never have a better pard
But you can't do that on the ground
So don't just sit there and fester
C'mon. Get up. Dust yourself off
And dance with me Mister

C'mon. Get up
We're just getting started
This job you took on yourself
Ain't for the timid hearted
I'll balk, I'll kick, I'll spin just like a Texas twister
So get up. Climb aboard and
Dance with me Mister

When I was born, I ran free
I didn't wear all this tack
I'm not about to give that up
For no gunsel or some hack

You got to prove to me you're worth it,
That you ain't just some weak sister.
So get up. Dust yourself off and show me what you got
C'mon. Dance with me Mister

Doused
~~ Harold Losey — ©2014 ~~

Do you remember Skeet?
Yes sir, he's our cow dog,
Still mostly at my feet.

Yup, he goes gets them beeves.
Avoiding all those hooves
As 'round the herd he weaves.

I let him out last night,
Right afore I turned in.
His barking was a fright!

Pulling on my jacket,
I wondered why Ole Skeet
Was raising such racket?

Skeet was by the tack shack,
And just a raisin' hell.
Might be a Diamondback.

That wouldn't be too strange.
So, I called for old Skeet,
To get him out of range.

Told Skeet he had to stay
And went to check it out.
Moved a bale from my way.

That pole cat shot its stuff,
And son, its aim was good.
My Lord the stink was rough

Why Skeet didn't get sprayed,
I doubt I'll ever know?
It could be that he prayed.

Three days since I got skunked
And I don't blame the boys.
That the barn's where I'm bunked.

Hey Country
~~ Harold Losey — ©2014 ~~

Have you ever been called "Country"?
Or how about just "Cowboy"?
Did you think it was peasantry?
Or was your heart filled with joy?

To be country or a cowboy
Takes a special kind of man.
A John Deere tractor's his first toy,
And a saddle his divan.

He'd wake 'fore the dawn is breakin'
Every day, all year long.
Try to give a fair accountin'
Not doing any man wrong.

Love of family, God and country,
Are this man's driving forces.
Handed down from his ancestry,
As is his love of horses.

The country boy's a gentleman,
And a scholar when he tries.
Shows respect for his fellow man,
Tells "tall tales", but never lies!

He works the land as he knows best,
Whether the boss or a hand.
Living by the "Code of the West"
Ev'ry day, "Ride for the Brand".

Finally his time draws to an end,
His steps short, friends a plenty.
Never had a need to pretend,
Cowboy Heaven a certainty.

If you are such a gentleman,
And with these facts you agree.
You will do whatever you can,
To hear folks call "Hey country".

Bunkhouse Porch
~~ Harold Losey — ©2013 ~~

They gather at the bunkhouse,
To have a little fun.
From cowboy to the cooks louse,
When their day's work is done.

They come to hear a new tale,
Or join the sing along.
Yarns spun on the cowboy trail,
Often retold through song.

Some tales are of cattle drives,
Others are of horses.
Some the feats of cowboy's lives,
Others nature's forces.

Most these tales been told before,
Some are made up brand new.
Many make your spirits soar,
Yet others you just rue.

There's always one old cowboy,
Whose tales can weave a spell.
He tells of a new colt's joy,
Or of a snow storm's hell.

The songs they might be ribald,
And cowgirls might just blush.
But when the last yarn is drawled,
"Good Night" prayer brings a hush.

My Home
~~ Harold Losey — ©2013 ~~

The city has its buildings,
Some seem to reach the sky.
Visitors look up in awe,
Not often knowing why.

City streets are loud and jammed.
Their volume doesn't drop.
Taxis' horns and buses' fumes,
This country boy yells STOP.

My home has its mountain tops,
And they do reach the sky.
They climb right into the clouds.
God made them that is why.

Visitors look up in awe,
God makes my sky so blue.
They wonder at the eagles,
As they soar into view.

My valleys are so peaceful,
And empty at first glance.
But soon you hear the bird's song,
And see the mule deer prance.

My rivers run fresh and pure.
The air is crisp and clean.
It might take your breath away,
The vista is so green.

Diamonds fill my skies at night.
The wolves sing me their song.
I reach out to touch the moon.
Sleep comes before too long.

The morning sun wakes me.
I rise, my spirit free.
A new day lies before me,
Its wonders for to see.

Bullfighter
~~ Harold Losey — ©2013 ~~

The announcer's voice boomed out
Starting up this contest
The gate opened with a shout
Only one would be best.

Leaping back I let them by
But they turn just so quick
The big one, he seemed to fly
This "muley" was some pick.

That big one began to spin
The cowboy held on tight
To be thrown would be a sin
But somethin' wasn't right.

The rider'd gone into "the well"
His riding hand "hung up"
Now this cowboy was in "hell"
My time to "cowboy up"

Time the spin and make my leap
I grab the rope's tag end
It comes free in one clean sweep
Again the rider's friend

"Why fight those bulls?" friends all cry
"Why risk your life and limbs?"
"It ain't the pay" I reply
"I answer cowboys' hymns."

Cowboy Heaven
~~ Harold Losey — ©2013 ~~

Today I sat and wondered,
As I gazed up to the sky.
This thought I often pondered.
What would happen when I die?

Will I get up to heaven?
And if I do arrive there,
Will there be any horsemen?
Will a "two-step" fill the air?

Will there be a horse corral?
Will there be a cattle herd?
Is there a cowboy chorale?
With their western singing heard?

Will the spring bring a round-up?
Will the calves be branded "hot"?
Coffee is from a tin cup,
Use a rag to grab the pot.

Will there be a rodeo?
Will the broncos kick and buck?
Will I cowboy in that show?
Cowboy heaven, that's my luck!

Mariah
~~ Harold Losey — ©2013 ~~

Away out here they got a name
For rain and wind and fire
The rain is Tess, the fire Joe,
And they call the wind Mariah
        -- Sam Cooke

Plains grass waves straw brown,
Parched by the constant sun.
Heat lightning ignites,
Prairie fire begun.

Sparks becoming flames,
Mariah fans the blaze.
Blackened ashes left,
Buildings and fences raze.

Thick smoke billowing,
Deer, hares running ahead.
Some not fast enough,
Left behind, the charred dead.

Mariah is stilled,
The fire burns away.
Tess quenches earth's thirst,
Joe waits for a new day.

Branding
~~ Harold Losey — ©2013 ~~

Smoke curling upward
Coals glowing brightly
Horses waiting work
Chinches drawn tightly

Cowboy's spurs ring out
As they each take mount
Some to cut out calves
Others take the count

The mesquite fire burns
Heating twisted steel
The kicking calf bawls
At the hot brand's feel

The air's aroma
Singed hair and burned hide
Every calf branded
Weary cowboy pride

Aces Over Eights
(August 2, 1876)
~~ Harold Losey — ©2013 ~~

The table was set,
Five chairs spaced 'round.
All their guns were checked,
Their places found.

One was tall and gaunt,
Eyes dark and cold.
Next came the short one,
Dressed bright, and bold.

The third man sat next,
With glasses dark.
Man four came whistling,
As on a lark.

Last man wore a star,
And pistols paired.
With back to the doors,
He was just chaired.

The chips are counted,
And money paid.
Antis collected,
The shuffle made.

The game, five card stud.
First two cards dealt,
High hand starts the bet.
Money hits the felt.

Hands are won, some lost.
The "star's" last hand,
Aces over eights.
Hickok's last stand.

Cowboy
~~ Harold Losey — ©2013 ~~

He's six foot three,
Or he's five foot two.
A little like me,
A little like you.

He wears his suits,
And he wears his ties.
He wears boots and jeans,
And will till he dies.

He opens doors,
And he pulls out chairs.
Calls all ladies Ma'am,
Shows women he cares.

He works all day,
From dawn till sundown.
Don't matter to him,
If no one's around.

His home's his ranch,
Be it large or small.
His country's his love,
For her he'd give all.

No matter where,
North, South, East, or West.
Of man or woman,
They're about the best.

A Stetson hat
In a Jersey bar
Or a Houston club
With a mean guitar.

Like Gene and Roy
Or Wayne and Eastwood
Yankee or Rebel
Cowboy life is good.

Here's to Sippin' Velvet
~~ Charli Love – ©2014 ~~

Two little cowboys listen to wild stories of his past
Where he talks about the rodeos, memories that would last
He once was a top notch cowboy who competed with the best
Cheyenne, Houston, Pendleton where he'd put his talent to the test

He talked about Sippin' Velvet though smooth she'd never be
Bucking off cowboys here and there it was quite the sight to see
He spoke about the glory days with a twinkle in his eye
Reminiscing about his past as if a movie flashing by

The listening two little cowboys focus with all their might
Memorizing every detail that ol' cowboy would recite
Now who knows what little cowboys ponder one could only guess
But I bet those boys were ridin' ol' Sippin' Velvet at recess

See that ol' cowboy is their hero like him they'd strive to be
Just ridin' the circuits rank ol' broncs for all the world to see
Well now these two little cowboys ain't so little anymore
They are tearing down every road they are fighting for every score

They are following the footsteps of the man they dreamed to be
Because the hero in the story is their daddy you see
The man whose legacy inspired them with stories of fame
Now sits back so proudly as his boys carry on the family name

Rodeos Are His Home
~ Charli Love – ©2013 ~

One would say he's a drifter
He's a loner on his own
Though thousands come to see him
He is never quite alone

He will drive and drive for miles
Living out this dream of his
The great dream of being known
To be known for all he is

Because he is a cowboy
A cowboy he'll always be
Chasing that dream of stardom
And the life to just be free

His body may be broken
And his wallet just the same
He can never ever stop
'Cause a cowboy can't be tamed

Rodeo's an addiction
It's a drug just like the rest
It feeds upon your hunger
Your great need to be the best

And a hope to be better
And to become better known
He may be called a drifter
Or a loner on his own

Though thousands come to see him
He is never quite alone
But so little do they know
That rodeos are his home

You Listen To The Boss
~~ Susan Matley – ©2014 ~~

You listen to the boss.
The thick muffler that insulates your neck
from bitter cold was knit of oatmeal fleck
and packed with Christmas fudge from your mother.
You sit astride, bear the icy north'er

And listen to the boss.
No more holidays for this cattle crew.
It's calving time you're briefed on. Eight of you
transform from roundup rowdies to midwives,
charged to deliver, maternity-wise.

You listen to the boss.
Eight hands make four pairs in round-the-clock shifts
and everyone's on call. You'll search the drifts
to rescue stowed-away calves. When they bawl
from the brush it's an urgent rescue call.

You listen to the boss.
The first-time heifers are sure to need aid
and no matter how well your plans are laid
when throwing a calf they might throw a twist.
The thought of the chaos makes your eyes mist.

You listen to the boss.
The worst part: waiting for calving to start.
But once it comes, anxiety departs.
The work is brutal; some will not survive.
Heart full, a new year entered by new lives
makes you glad you listened to the boss.

Green Energy
~~ Susan Matley – ©2012 ~~

'Twas at the end of round up time.
Jake ponied his horses in line;
the four who'd served through autumn's lease
were done with work and bound for peace.

Lead lines to tails he tied his knots.
to the corral! (or so Jake thought)

With Jake astride and feeling pleased,
Scout strode mightily at the lead.
But Barney, Doc, and Big Cheese, last
were disinclined to go so fast.

"That show-off and his fancy prance,"
snorted second-in-line equine.
Scout winced, his tail yanked too dang hard
as lazy Barney lagged behind.

Barney that day had eaten green grass,
ears flat, he'd hogged the entire patch,
and puttered a methane stream behind.
That's when Doc gave a tug on the line.

Big Cheese dreamily watched the scenery,
when nose met flank he cursed Doc obscenely
and gave him a nip on the rear. The line
had veered too much for Jake. He held a fine,
wide cuss-word on his breath. "Whoa, Scout," he said,
wondering of what sires these boys were bred.
Shaking his head, he twisted to look aft;
long, grumpy faces regarded him back.

Dismounting, he ambled to the back of the train
for the simplest re-fit his thoughts could attain.
Swapping Doc to behind and Big Cheese to the third,
he continued the trek with his four-pony herd.

But with a fresh start, it didn't go easy:
big Cheese veered from side-to-side as if queasy,
a drag that none of his string-mates could master.
"What the heck?" Jake groaned. The range seemed far vaster
than ever with rebellion in the ranks.
As he swung down again, his patience shrank.

He bellowed, "Ponies, your attention, please!
Now follow Scout's lead, stop dreamin', Big Cheese,"
he grumbled as he switched Big Cheese with Barney,
"I've had enough of your air-headed blarney."

Jake assumed the saddle once more.
But in one hundred yards he swore;
Doc, taking a turn for the dramatic,
performed a prancing side-to-side antic.

"All right, all right!" Jake shouted in defeat.
"If this don't work," said he, as earth met feet,
"I'm gonna leave the string of you behind!"
Checking bad temper, he kept in his mind
their only hope was working as a team;
Barney moved rear in the ponied-up scheme.

To Jake's surprise, the last leg of their trip
made record time; they fairly seemed to rip
across the range, back to the ranch at last;
he never knew they were powered by gas.

Dust
~~ Susan Matley – ©2012 ~~

The world is blown monochrome,
Dusted in sepia tones.
High wind warning for today;
You race to bale the cut hay
Before it starts to fly.

The work day doesn't start
Until your teeth are full of grit.
Skin-cracking hours depart
As you hold a grin and bear it

When you can't quite see the cattle
As they mill around your saddle;
Just ghostly bovine highlights
In daylight gone twilight
With sun still in the sky.

Sweat lends dust an artistic hand,
Plasters your burnt hide in shades of gray,
Transforming you from mortal man
To living statue of desert clay.

When cattle work is done,
When the herd acts as one
And settles as if in concert,
The dust settles, too: common dirt.
Bits of sand on ground lie.

Tomorrow's dust will rise. You'll spend
Each day with grit that flies anew.
And as the dust that's how you'll end;
It's always been just dust and you.

Bleached Bones
~~ Susan Matley – ©2010 ~~

Forty miles from the saw mill
Near the Blues, in the foothills
By horse-drawn wagon borne:
Board lumber. Hard to find then,
In 1866 when
The little house was formed.

One room. Stove, table and bed
For man and wife, newly wed;
Threshold crossed in moon glow.
Two windows cut were dead eyes,
Deer skin cured to keep out flies.
The floor – - dirt, cool and low.

Time brought change, and babes a few.
With family the house grew,
A sunny porch enclosed.
A separate kitchen next,
More mouths to feed the pretext,
A wooden floor imposed.

The kids grew strong and grew fast,
Both boys and girls, 'til at last
One room per gender came.
A new room: the lady's pride.
Claw-foot bathtub moved inside
With white commode and chain.

The railroad came and town spread
To the farm. In social dread
The house blushed with new paint.
The elite sniffed, "Ramshackle."
But not too many cackled
Their houses, too, were quaint.

And then the railroad died, and
The town did slowly disband.
Off to cities most fled.
Man and wife grew old and tired,
Their kids in city jobs admired,
Earning their daily bread.

The house that grew couldn't shrink
And the kids began to think
Mom and Dad should retreat.
The farm was sold, the house fell
Silent, fading in the hell
Of love grown obsolete.

The Patch
~~ Debra Meyer – ©2009 ~~

This trail that I ride runs on ahead,
Though I can't quite see round the bend.
I once thought this trail everlastin',
But now I'm aware there's an end.

I pause to reflect and look backward,
At the course I've already run,
It's littered with heartbreak and laughter,
Things 'complished and things left undone.

That stretch yet to ride's a might shorter,
Than the miles that I've left behind,
But I tote some dreams in my pocket,
There's a place I'm longin' to find.

A good patch of ground's what I yearn for,
Though time trots on by me it seems.
Knee-deep in thick sweetgrass I'll find it,
A place where I'll shake out my dreams.

I'll build me a house to come home to,
A barn for my horses and hay.
I'll work on the patch until evenin',
Then rest at the closin' of day.

I'll gather my loved ones around me,
We'll watch for the sunlight's last beams.
I'll tell them the story of one man,
Whose loop was tied fast to his dreams.

"Was it hard?" they will ask, and I'll smile,
Nod my head and give it a scratch.
"It was hard, but all worth the doin'
A man's got to have him a patch."

I rein in the thoughts jiggin' round me,
Then turn to continue the ride.
I pack up my dreams in my pocket,
And button them safely inside.

There ain't many things that I'm sure of,
I count no chicks before the hatch,
But I trust that God and good horses,
Will carry me on t'ward my patch.

Hard Candy Cowboy
~~ *Debra Meyer* – ©2009 ~~

He wasn't large in stature,
Couldn't tell it by his walk.
His bobwire eyes could cut you,
Had no nonsense in his talk.

Some folks, they'd shy around him,
Cause he came off sorta gruff,
Made no bones 'bout right 'n wrong,
And he'd tell it to you rough.

His body bore the traces,
Of the trade he'd made his own,
He took up bronco bustin',
When he wasn't quite full-grown.

His hands was scarred and twisted,
Not a finger there was straight.
His legs was bowed and crooked,
Had a wobble in his gait.

He built a reputation,
Over forty years or so,
For turnin' out good horses,
Both for workin' and for show.

I sometimes came to watch him,
But took heed in what folks said.
"Stay out the way and quiet,
Or that man'll have your head."

The horses that they brung him,
Was the rankest ones to ride.
Most had been treated spiteful,
Wore the proof upon their hide.

I watched him with the horses,
He was tough, but not unkind.
He made the right choice easy,
So the wrong was left behind.

"These horses took their troubles,
Not from nature, but from man."
His words were strong and steady,
"I just do the best I can.

I put the trust back in 'em,
That another took away."
I saw him stroke the forelock,
Of a little Arab bay.

A man's soul can't be hidden,
From the creatures in his care.
The horses knew the secret,
That the cowboy wouldn't share.

I watched the cowboy workin'
And I quickly struck a thought,
I was thinkin' bout hard candies,
That my mamma sometimes bought.

Their flavor was strawberry,
A right tasty sort of treat,
On the outside hard and sour,
But the inside's soft and sweet.

That cowboy and them candies,
Both were filled with a surprise.
The hard and sour outside,
Was used only for disguise.

I liked those 'berry candies,
Came to like that cowboy too.
Forever in my memory,
That hard candy buckaroo.

Heartache and Pards
~~ Debra Meyer – ©2013 ~~

His words were plain and to the point,
"Sometimes this life just sucks.
She does her best to throw ya down,
She boogers and she bucks."

The cowboy knew the trail I rode,
The steep and rocky way.
I came for lies and platitudes,
But truth was all he'd say.

"You're gonna hurt a good long time,
Ain't nothin' can be done.
You'll ride awhile in blackest night,
Before ya see the sun.

"The pain you feel ain't nothin' new.
Just look around, and know,
That scores of riders up ahead,
Have passed the way you'll go."

His thoughts were far from comforting,
Not what I came to hear.
His kindness smoothed their edges though,
And helped to calm my fear.

"There's some will buckle to the test,
Some barely make it through.
But you, you're tough. You'll be just fine.
I've seen what you can do.

"Remember that I'll be right here,
When livin' feels too hard.
If ever you should need a friend,
Just holler for yer pard."

Wooin' the Mule
~~ Debra Meyer – ©2010 ~~

I's up to Ed's one Sunday,
We was plannin' on a ride.
I hollered at his barn door,
Then I moseyed on inside.

My eyes just took a smidgeon
To adjust to dimmer light.
N' I found that I was peerin'
At a most engagin' sight.

Dappled gray with great long ears,
Pickin' hay there in a stall.
One quick glance he cast my way,
Then the mule turned t'ward the wall.

"Must be shy," I says to Ed,
As I offer up a rub.
He turned again, deliberate,
And I took it as a snub.

"One fine judge of character!"
Ed was chucklin' as he spoke.
"They's some he just don't take to,
Guess you ain't his kind of folk."

"What's that to mean?" I queried.
"Not his kind of folk, indeed!"
And then as if to comment,
The mule stretched hisself and peed.

"He just needs time to know me,"
I spoke up on my behalf.
"I'll get a chair," Ed spluttered,
No attempt to hide his laugh.

I sat and watched the south end
Of a northern-facin' john.
I'd prove that I was worthy;
I was one to count upon.

"Just consider this, my friend,"
We debated as I sat.
"I'm good and kind," I told him,
As he dodged another pat.

I then began some sweet talk,
Even tried to share my chuck.
His negative reaction,
Made me cuss and damn my luck.

The words I strung together,
Would have served a sailor well.
"Told you so," Mule seemed to snort.
"You'll be goin' straight to hell!"

That fiery accusation,
Made me pause and look within.
It seemed my knack fer cussin',
Wasn't near my greatest sin.

I am a might impatient.
I've been knowed to take a drink.
'N' I'm quick to get a mad on.
Mule agreed, with gaseous stink.

"You're right," I then conceded.
"I'm unworthy and a fool."
I was judged a sinner and,
Out-debated by a mule.

Horse Sense
~~ Debra Meyer – ©2012 ~~

"She's strong," the cowboy offered,
With a twinkle in his eye.
"I'll wager she's got bottom,
With no quit and lots of try."

I glanced in the direction
That his nod bid me to go.
"Purty head, a real nice neck,
She looks fine enough to show."

"I betcha she ain't cold-backed,
Like some others I have knowed.
She's fit and not too fleshy."
Words of praise pert nearly flowed.

I gaped in pure confusion,
At a hammer-headed mare.
She'd been around the range some,
You could plainly see the wear.

Her pig eyes stared out blankly,
Her old cowhocks nearly kissed,
The faults I seen was endless,
They's too numerous to list.

The cowboy had horse savvy.
His pronouncements took as law,
But the crazy he was talkin'
Worked my brain 'til it was raw.

A fever might a took'im
Or his eyes was gettin' dim.
I's scramblin' for the answer,
When I stopped and looked at him.

No squintin' nor a'quakin'
So I knew I had to ask.
"Pard," I queried cautiously,
"Ya been emptyin' yer flask?"

His gaze was straight and level,
As he looked me in the eye.
"Nope," was all he said to me,
But his count'nance added "why?"

I spluttered and I stammered,
Tried in vain to find my voice.
I didn't want to tell him,
But there clearly weren't no choice.

"Well," I started nervously,
Tryin' hard not to affront.
"That hoss ain't naught but crowbait!"
Hadn't meant to be so blunt.

"A greenhorn ought not question,
The fine wisdom I bestow."
The cowboy was a'smilin',
Talkin' soft and kinda slow.

His grin kept gettin' bigger,
Till it lit the whole corral.
"Ne'er said it were the mare, son.
I was talkin' 'bout the gal."

A purty senorita,
Led that nag on out the gate.
He watched as she departed,
"Looky there, she's trackin' straight."

The Right Lead
~~ Debra Meyer – ©2012 ~~

He stood there in the dust and dirt,
Sweat drippin' down his face.
"What is it you cain't understand?"
He then began to pace.

The bristly hairs upon his head,
(The ones that still remained),
Swirled crazily about his ears,
His countenance was pained.

"The leads you take start at the hind,
Then end up with the fore.
You've got to set your horse up right."
He paused, then, offered more.

"To get the left, you cue the right,
For right, it is reversed."
I watched him stride across the sand.
His speech was well rehearsed.

I tried my best to catch each word,
Translate them to my steed.
Again, I asked him for a right
But, got that damned left lead.

I tried at least a dozen more,
With similar result.
The trainer's eyes shot t'ward the sky
For heavenly consult.

"Well then," he said, "we'll try the fence.
This has to work, you'll see.
Just run him at an angle with
Degrees of thirty-three."

"The moment that you reach the fence,
The left leg gives a squeeze,
The right leg lifts the shoulder up."
His orders flew with ease.

"Push your inside seatbone forward,
The reins up t'wards his poll,
Tip his head to the outside edge,
Sit deep and let it roll!"

Though the trainer thought this simple,
My brain was chuggin' quick.
Keepin' up with his directions
Was harder than a brick.

Was my inside seatbone forward?
The angle thirty-three?
I was runnin' through the checklist,
As ready as I'd be.

"Do it now!" the trainer bellowed.
I took off like a shot.
Was the right lead in my future?
The left lead's what I got.

"Wrong lead," he sounded weary.
A tear formed in his eye.
We both hoped not to hear it, but
He whispered, "One more try."

That 'one more try' turned into ten.
My trainer had some grit.
He was sick and tired of preachin',
But never did he quit.

He took it from the top again,
The A to Z of leads,
Just yearnin' for the harvest since,
He'd planted scores of seeds.

His wits was workin' overtime.
To find out what was missin'.
The answer finally popped in place,
Some folks just don't listen.

For me the lesson is quite clear:
When next that I should ride,
Instead of askin' for a lead,
I'll let the horse decide.

Writers of the Purple Sage
~~ *LTC Roy E. Peterson* — ©*2013* ~

What happened to the music? The writers of the West?
The legends of the cowboys? The songs that I love best?
The outlaws and the posse? Please tell me where they went?
The ones who shared their stories of will and testament.

I think that Marty Robbins is stuck in El Paso
A ghost in the cantina, where Rosa loved him so.
Grandsons of the Pioneers must be great grandpas now.
I think that they've forgotten the Westerns anyhow.

Gene Autry went to heaven. He got a second chance.
He got a million acres; a new Melody Ranch.
I searched through Apple Valley for Gabby, Dale, and Roy,
But their stuff was carted off to Branson by his boy.

The last I heard of Willie, he sang a song with Ray
Of Seven Spanish Angels that saw a fight one day.
"When the battle stopped and … there was thunder from the throne.
Seven Spanish Angels took another angel home."

Tex Ritter and Rex Allen, Jim Reeves, and Frankie Laine
The singers of the Westerns I'd love to hear again.
The Yellow Rose of Texas, the Rose of San Antone
How well do I remember those memories etched in stone.

Go find a singing cowboy and find a pretty lass
And write for them some music out of our Western past.
The Western told the legends they sang up on the stage.
Where are Western writers; Writers of the Purple Sage?

[The final two lines of the fourth stanza are from the song "Seven Spanish Angels," a 1984 single written by Troy Seals and Eddie Setser and recorded by Willie Nelson and Ray Charles.]

Tucson Sunday Morning
~~ *LTC Roy E. Peterson – ©1974 & 2006* ~~

(Chorus) Tucson Sunday morning, see the sage brush come alive.
Gold upon the Rincons, Catalina mountain sides.
Saguaro in the desert lift their silent arms in prayer.
The mission bell is tolling, my stage will soon be rolling,
But my dreams will still be there.

Cantina of Alinda, where I bedded for a while.
Was it the fiery liquor, or the senorita's smile.
Warm nights with soft Alinda. Palo Verde scented hair.
When I awoke it was the dawn and I had to travel on,
But my dreams will still be there. (Chorus Repeat)

They found another Marshall. Said he's riding in today.
It's time that I was leaving for the border anyway.
The vision of Alinda with a flower in her hand
Will bring me back some midnight when the moon is shining bright
On the Tucson golden sand. (Chorus Repeat)

Gunfighter's life is anguish, always danger in the air.
I headed for Alinda, though I knew I shouldn't dare.
Tucson streets were empty; caught a flash of forty-four.
Is that really you Alinda? Am I at your hacienda?
Is that my body lying there? (Chorus Repeat)

[From the author's books: Between Darkness and Light and American Heritage Poetry Collection.]

Dogies in Our Band
~ Tom Swearingen — © 2014 ~

In every band of livestock
You might find a few that's weak
Some through trouble at their birth
Their prospects are most times bleak

Some weakened by lack of food
Or poor shelter in bad climes
Or accident or sickness
Motherless calves often times

"Dogies" is what you call them
They're the trailers in the band
First to suffer, fade, and die
When some hardship hits the land

"Dogies" just like in the song
"Little dogies git along
Your misfortune not my own
Little dogies git along"

And so it is with people
We've sure got some dogies too
Those driftin' through misfortune
So just what are we to do?

Do we just say "git along
Your misfortune not our own
Git along little dogie
You just drift along alone"?

No, I say if we're able
We extend a helping hand
Their misfortune is our own
'Cause we're part of the same band

You of course do what you will
And I'll do what I decide
But if you were the dogie
You'd want someone at your side

A Winter Pleasure Ride
~~ *Tom Swearingen – © 2013* ~~

We started out with slickers
On or carried just in case
Wild rags tied to warm our neck
Or to pull up on our face

Layered up with woolies on
Two shirts and a heavy vest
And blanket-lined canvas coats
Figured that should stand the test

Now past three the skies are dark
And the wind is blowing mean
The forecast folks reporting
We're due squall like we've not seen

Yet, we're on a "pleasure ride"
'Least we say that's what we do
Hard to 'magine that today
With this big 'ol storm 'a brew

'Cause all the time we're riding
That sun has been getting low
The temperature's been falling
Eating at our inner glow

Our cheeks are getting tingly
And our noses have a run
This little "ride for pleasure"
Why, she's stopping to be fun

So we ride in to the wind
Find our way back to the road
Then in the barn unsaddle
Warm, and get the tack all stowed

Later with the horses groomed
We reflect upon our ride
Was that a ride "for pleasure"?
"It sure was" we all decide

Because time in the saddle
Is what we've come to treasure
Don't matter the conditions
We'll always find some pleasure

Be that pleasure of senses
Those, the seeing touching kind
Or pleasure that takes place deep
In the thinking of a mind

Just give us time with horses
And as long as we're astride
Won't matter what's encountered
We'll make it a "pleasure ride"

The Mystery of Superstition Mountain
~~ Tom Swearingen – ©2012 ~~

East of Apache Junction
You see it standing grand
Jutting some three thousand feet
'Top Arizona sand

"Superstition Mountain", so
How did it get that name?
Did it bring some good fortune
Or increase luck or fame?

Does the name reflect hardship,
Or loss from days of old?
Maybe that of the miners
Who dug the rock for gold?

Why, people are looking yet
For that Lost Dutchman Mine
Its mother lode still hidden
Away from bright sunshine

No, I am told the name comes
From much more ancient days
From lore of native Pimas,
Or from Apache braves

"Bad medicine" they called wind
That howled down from the spires
Their fear of mountain's spirits
Long shared around their fires

So when early settlers came
And heard those Indian tales
About lower worlds believed
Behind the mountain's wails

They called them "superstitious"
So, there's the history
But while that explains the name
There's still a mystery

Is there some truth behind what
Those Indian legends say?
And if so, are the spirits
Still with us here today?

First Night in Arizona
~~ Tom Swearingen – ©2012 ~~

Seventy-five Kent reports
And nary a cloud at all
But here it is November
Two full months now into fall

Envious? Hard to not be
Why just look there at the shot
The photo that he sent us
Of their winter livin' spot

First eve of their arrival
In the Arizona sun
They're riding in the desert
Many miles from Oregon

That Saguaro by Linda
Must be thirty plus feet high
A great spire of succulence
Long arms reaching to the sky

Linda's bay Paint Horse Seven
Looks curiously content
Wonder if she's wondering
Where the Douglas Firs all went

Not missing a minute though
The wet ground she left back home
'Cause now there's miles of dry sand
And gravelly earth to roam

Yep, they've done traded soft mud
And slop splashed up to the hocks
For bone dry hooves, dusty legs
And sure-footed sunbaked rocks

It's a swap we could go for
And someday just might arrange
Leave Oregon for winters
On the Arizona range

I'm anxious for what they say
When our friends come back in spring
Find out if their maiden trip
Will become their annual thing

But I am pretty certain
That I know just what they'll say
It's right there in the photo
As clear as a sunny day

You just look at Linda's smile
Tell me that don't say it all
Gleaming, beaming, happiness
I'm sure they'll head back come fall

Horses and Happiness
~~ Tom Swearingen – ©2013 ~~

Money can't buy happiness
You've heard that saying ring
But money can buy horses
And that's the same dang thing

Buy a horse and you'll agree
My observation's true
Might just be the finest thing
You'll likely ever do

That horse will bring you comfort
A thousand pounds of friend
Bring hours of enjoyment
On that you can depend

Sure, you'll say "So long, money!"
That truth I will concede
But you will barely miss it
Spend'n it on your steed

Money can't buy happiness
At least that's what they say
But money can buy horses
I'll take that any day

Blessed to be Western
~~ Tom Swearingen – ©2013 ~~

How did those early settlers
To the west get this far
With no Map Quest or smart phone
Or Tom Tom in their car?

Well, some followed directions
They'd gotten from someone
Some dead reckoned by the stars
Or shadows of the sun

Some they came by dumb blind luck
Or hired on a guide
Others joined in with the crowd
And come in with the tide

It's somethin' that they came west
Not sure just what they'd find
Or even how to get here
Left all their world behind

No matter how they got here
Or what gave them the fire
I'm glad my kin came out west
And sparked in me desire

To ride the open prairies
And over mountain trails
To love western heritage
And all that it entails

Thank's for set'lin in the west
And planting my roots here
I am blessed to be western
It's all that I hold dear

Nightwind. Gentle Spirit, Noble Soul
~~ Tom Swearingen – ©2013 ~~

Twenty two years. A good long time
To spend with an equine friend
So, there's no getting around
Sadness when coming to the end

Good night Nightwind. We'll miss you girl
Time you just rest peaceful now
Won't be the same without you here
But we'll get through it somehow

I expect you'll often find us
Out lingering by your grave
Recalling all the good times
We had and memories to save

We'll be listn'n for your nicker
In the rustling of the trees
And the call of your whinny
In the soft whistle of the breeze

Then in the evening darkness
We will scan the far fence line
And imagine your outline
Walking and you'll be doing fine!

Sound as you were when we showed you
And we rode the trails for miles
Or took kids on their first rides
And you gave 'em all such big smiles

We'll take comfort in our mem'ry
Now you rest your noble soul
Rest easy gentle spirit
For there are no more miles to go

When a Horse Hoof Hits the Ground
~~ Tom Swearingen — ©2013 ~~

I hear something special when a horse hoof hits the ground
Nothing else as magic as the rhythm of that sound

Whether just a gentle clip clop ambling down a street
Or thunder at the gallop just a blur of legs and feet

Don't matter if it's barefoot or shod with nails and steel
There's nothing else I've heard that gives me quite the feel

I've heard the greatest orchestras and a diva's glorious song
And choirs harmonizing like a grand angelic throng

I've seen the late and great ones from Elvis to George Jones
Those with voices that move and shake you deep down to your bones

But I hear something special when a horse hoof hits the ground
Nothing else as magic as the rhythm of that sound

I've heard a child's first words and the whinny of a new born foal
And beautiful songs of yesteryear and classic poems of ol'

The echo through the canyon of coyotes checking in
And the gentle sound of evening breeze at daylight's peaceful end

Yes those sounds are wonderful and each speaks to my soul
But so does the sound of hoof beats when horses are on the roll

Yes, I hear something special when a horse hoof hits the ground
Nothing else as magic as the rhythm of that sound

When I listen to those hoof beats no telling what I'll find
With imagination running free painting pictures in my mind

A future derby winner leading on the rail
A Pony Express rider rushing someone's mail

A Finals barrel racer turning on a dime
The old country doctor's buggy arriving just in time

A desperado's getaway following a spree
The posse hot behind aiming to hang him in a tree

A bred to buck saddle bronc flanked and just set loose
A proud Umatilla Indian on a swift Cayuse

Or the horses I grew up with when I was just a pup
Fury, Silver, Trigger, and my stick horse Giddy-Up

No telling where they'll take me when I hear a horse's feet
My imagination up in the saddle riding with the beat

Yeah, I hear something special when a horse hoof hits the ground
Nothing else as magic as the rhythm of that sound

Going to the Rodeo
~ *J. Wesley Taylor, Sr. – ©2009* ~

There are choices we all make in life.
One day I chose to watch a rodeo;
What amazing things I did sit and watch,
I knew it was a place that I should go.

I watched a cowboy with a Stetson hat
and he was riding on a bronco's back
while it was jumping, prancing, all around.
Within this day, of fun there was no lack.

I heard as they announced the next event;
this one was a delightful bareback ride.
A cowgirl on its back, it jumped around
and with tightened knees she had lotsa pride.

Great entertainment in this western state,
exciting times that came with each event.
We all saw bucking bulls and running steers
and we enjoyed the times that came and went.

I looked and saw some barrels standing there,
I sat while waiting for a barrel race.
Then as I watched I saw some barrels fall
and yet I saw, each horse did keep its pace.

Then the time did come for a stampede run,
with horses charging past the entrance gate.
While moving in a circle, side by side,
they then picked up their speed to not be late.

When we saw everything that came along
we really loved it when we saw each clown.
While doing just the job they knew was theirs,
protecting cowboys who were falling down.

My thoughts now roam through all those things I saw,
and even though it is a passing day,
I have mem'ries that now do dwell within,
I also see those words, "hooray, hooray!"

A Texas Picnic
~~ *J. Wesley Taylor, Sr. – ©2008* ~~

A covered wagon went one day
to take my mama out to play.
Her pappy drove the oxen there,
they knew his heart was filled with care.
My mama told me, don't you see?

'T were miles away from Austin town
and her two brothers came on down.
The wagon carried quite a load
as they went on an old dirt road.
Way out in Texas, don't you see?

All three were there with ma and pa,
in wonder of those things they saw
that brightened 'neath the sunny sky
and brought them smiles as they passed bye.
Out in the country, don't you see?

They passed on through an old dry crick
to reach a place for their picnic.
The wagon was a place of shade
while resting from the games they played.
A place of comfort, don't you see?

Their ma and pa prepared the food
and it had tasted o' so good.
It seems like there was quite a bunch
of stuff that they could sit and munch.
Just yummy, yummy, don't you see?

As night drew near their pa did climb
where he could find a strong tree limb
to build a place where they could sleep
and through the night their safety keep.
    A time of safety, don't you see?

Those times at night they all might hear
the sounds of wolves who wandered near.
It seems those wolves would come to howl
as closely they did come to prowl.
        Way out in Texas, don't you see?

Then as the morning time would come
the wagon then would take them home
with all those mem'ries they could hold
as though their day was filled with gold.
        My mama told me, don't you see?
        Way out in Texas, don't you see?

A New Land
~~ J. Wesley Taylor, Sr. – ©1962 ~~

Because they wanted room to breathe
And deep within their breasts did seethe
A will to live as free men should,
To give their children all things good,
They set forth to find ... A NEW LAND.

Setting sail o'er windswept sea
Unto a land where man is free;
Within their hearts a dream they keep
And brave each peril of the deep,
To set foot upon ... A NEW LAND.

Yet the perils do not cease
Although each man would live in peace.
The price of freedom ... blood and tears,
Then toil and sweat throughout the years.
This is the cost of ... A NEW LAND.

Then west unto the mountains tall
To answer there the beck'ning call.
Upon each homestead cabins raise
Yet still unto the West they gaze,
Eyes straining t'ward ... A NEW LAND.

Onward to the West they trod
O'er dusty earth and sun baked sod,
Through freezing night and scorching day
That they might ever find the way
Leading them unto ... A NEW LAND.

Man's search for freedom never ends
And thus it is he ever wends
His way unto an unknown place
O'er desert, sea, and into space
Ever searching for ... A NEW LAND.

Snake Oil
~~ *D. Weaver* – ©2013 ~~

Charlie was sound asleep that night
layin' on the prairie ground
resting there beside the campfire
and not makin' any sound

We had watched the snake slither in
we reckoned he liked the heat
knowin' it wouldn't be too long
'til old Charlie found his feet

Bets were made how long it'd take
for Charlie to come alive
we moved to give him plenty room
to make that frightening dive

When that varmit wound 'round his leg
and cuddled up close to him
the world seemed to explode 'round us
his face was a'lookin' grim

Charlie made one great gallant hop
and then came back down to earth
he turned over twice while up there
cactus would be his next curse

He landed on them sticky thorns
the snake still around his leg
then went again t'ward the heavens
kinda' like a powderkeg

The cowboys were a'hollerin'
they were dancin' up a jig
we never seen nothin' like it
cause the bets were gettin' big

Now we knew that snake was harmless
he didn't have no rattle
to Charlie he was a killer
and put up quite a battle

To say if he was skeered to death
it would make a lizard blush
surely it was just some bad luck
to land in a thorny brush

That badger that he fell upon
was a little bit upset
went to scratchin' and bitin' him
soon we all began to fret

We felt that we might still save him
was in a lotta' trouble
me 'n Billy Gant jumped right in
'midst all that thorny stubble

That badger was still a'fumin'
he bit Billy on his hand
the snake had abandoned Charlie
then to me he meant to brand

It was then I saw the button
right at the end of his tail
somehow he done lost his rattles
so I soon began to wail

My thoughts was how bad I'd suffer
when in me he put them fangs
I was cryin' like a baby
just like a coyote sangs

The cowboys watched in sheer horror
were certain that I would die
why, even a couple of them
broke down and began to cry

Suddenly my miracle came
the old badger et that snake
he ran away as Charlie left
it was then I came awake

Now I'm afraid to sleep again
this 'un was a bad nightmare
drank me a pot of spiked coffee
what was in it I don't care

Joe Wilson
~~ D. Weaver — © 2014 ~~

Old Joe Wilson was feelin' bad
as he swept the barroom floor
He'd drank himself to sleep last night
woke up early wantin' more

The town drunk for nigh' on ten years
cleans out the stables each morn'
Works at the bar for his whiskey
folks laugh as his heart is torn

At one time he was respected
it seems a lifetime ago
Owned a big ranch and lovely home
a wife and two boys to grow

The typhus took them in the spring
and he lost his mind and soul
Rode away and gave up the ranch
the sorrow then took it's toll

There's nights you hear his lonely cry
it comes from his soul inside
He dreams of a time long ago
before his family died

The town's banker makes sport of him
there's a sneer upon his lips
Embarassment is his weapon
smiles as he makes funny quips

Joe picks up a quarter that's thrown
by the banker man himself
Joe makes his way to the saloon
takes a bottle from the shelf

The next day two boys are playin'
in the middle of the street
A runaway stage comes flyin'
they freeze and fail to retreat

Only Joe see's the danger come
and dashes to them to help
He pushes each to safety then
as the horses give a yelp

There on the street lies his body
he died there under the stage
Joe Wilson now rests on Boot Hill
'mongst the cactus and the sage

They put up a stone monument
to honor the one who gave
He lies with his family now
with fresh flowers on his grave

The man who brings those fresh flowers
works down at the local bank
He's the father of those two boys
he has only Joe to thank

People of the Prairie
~~ *D. Weaver* — © *2014* ~~

The roar of the Sharps' fifty-caliber
echoes around the rolling hills
The last bull of the small buffalo herd
lies alone as his lifeblood spills

The rest of the little herd lie scattered
along the prairie's vast expanse
The carcasses lay where they have fallen
with no ceremonial dance

Their huge hides are the only things taken
while the rest is wasted away
Native tribes are now unable to hunt
the winter will bring much dismay

The white man brings untold decimation
for the Native Indian bands
All but a few never understanding
while taking the tribes sacred lands

A lone Indian sits on his pony
on a small hill not far away
Lost in thought as he solemnly sits there
gazing at the gruesome display

In his heart is a deep and dark sadness
his people were taken and bound
In his eyes there is no whisper of hope
and a teardrop falls to the ground

Cowboy Larry & Ol' Stick
~~ D. Weaver — © 2014 ~~

It was early in the mornin'
when he rode into town
He tied his pony at the rail
and stumbled to the ground

He asked us if he had fallen
we told him not a chance
Not darin' to make fun of him
with his clothes all askance

We snickered at his wood pony
with his leg near wore off
Slowly hobbled onto the porch
ignored us with our scoff

Hitchin' up his baggy britches
strode into the saloon
Ordered six shots of buttermilk
and drank 'til afternoon

Proclaimed that his name was Larry
and came to ride "Old Fred"
The meanest bronc who ever lived
who filled cowboys with dread

We asked about his wood pony
how he come to own him
"I won him in a poker game
and liked his only limb"

He ordered up more buttermilk
for all who had gathered
Slowly tossed up his empty glass
with cap gun he shattered

The ladies workin' upstairs screamed
one came out and hollered
Larry then bowed and tipped his hat
strange the scene that follered

She giggled as he slipped and fell
upon those schards of glass
He rebounded into the air
like an atomic blast

Flipped over twice then back to earth
sharp glass in ever' place
He then lit into a cussin'
to him she did embrace

Larry was no simple pilgrim
when his hat was on straight
Stood there like a rodeo clown
this gal would be his fate

A thousand bucks went to the man
who rode this old cayuse
He could buck like no other bronc
dishin' out much abuse

The greatest desire filled his heart
to ride this outlaw Fred
Said I'll just ride this nag for sure
or I'll drop over dead

We hoorayed at the way he walked
he never said a word
Then walked on by the rest of us
just like he never heard

The horse that he was lookin' for
was in chute number nine
Larry walked up very slowly
then patted his behind

We thought he must have gone crazy
he opened up that gate
'cause standin' there just a waitin'
twelve hundred pounds of hate

The buckskin tried to run him down
but Larry was too quick
He threw his arms around his neck
like it was some old trick

Pulled hisself upon Old Fred's back
as if he was a cat
Calmly sat like he was born there
in his white Stetson hat

Fred came out with his hind-end up
his front end on the ground
Just kickin' hard and squeelin' loud
tryin' to shake 'im down

The cowboy didn't give an inch
rode wherever he went
Rode him down 'til he couldn't move
Fred was finally spent

The buckskin stood there a'blowin'
ashamed that he'd been rode
By a skinny worn-out cowboy
nobody even knowed

Larry un-horsed from that buckskin
proudly waved to the crowd
They stood up and cheered him wildly
he nodded and then bowed

Larry turned his back on Old Fred
never suspecting harm
Fred took him hard on his shoulder
nearly breaking his arm

He fell to the rodeo ground
Fred tried his best to kill
Ol' Larry rolled into a ball
the crowd it brung a chill

A hush then came over the crowd
they watched in disbelief
His stick-horse then came a'hoppin'
to give him some relief

He saved the cowboy's life that day
fightin' there with Old Fred
Kicked him with that old wooden leg
'til most thought he was dead

Cowboy Larry took his money
we don't know where he went
Took with him a lovely lady
a wedding she'd consent

So the moral of this story
don't sell a stick-horse short
'cause sometimes it's the little things
that make us laugh and snort

The High Drive
~ D. Weaver – ©2012 ~

The sun was shinin' e'er so bright
as we left camp that morn'
Jack had brewed up some coffee strong
watchin' a calf get born

That little guy struggled right up
and tried his best to walk
Jack had took a likin' to him
and watched him 'round the clock

Me and Jack were ridin' partners
been together for years
just two ornery old cowboys
with a great thirst for beers

Our lives were spent tendin' the herd
all we knew how to do
we had signed on for a new drive
in just a week or two

We were headin' toward the north
Montana we would dare
'Good Lord a' mercy' Jack burst out
we'll freeze to death up there

The trail boss said get ready boys
best pack up all your gear
Jack got a blanket for the calf
warmth for the new frontier

He called that newborn calf Walter
we all dared not to laugh
Jack cared for him like a baby
he was his chosen calf

He knew the cowboys were funnin'
and fed him small tidbits
our old cook was gettin' upset
Jack was sneakin' biscuits

Walter became our new mascot
ridin' cross Jack's saddle
if somebody didn't like it
no doubt they'd do battle

The calf was growin' up nicely
becomin' quite a steer
the way Jack cared for him each day
sometimes it brung a tear

The new trail was hot and dusty
at first we started out
the cows took time to settle in
at first they scattered 'bout

Walter mingled with the cattle
his coat a brown and white
dancin' and playin' among them
he was a handsome sight

The days started to get cooler
we sang cowboy anthems
we only lost two steers out there
Boss threw coupla' tantrums

Wyoming proved to be harder
badlands tested our crew
the weaker cows were a'struggling
we only lost a few

At last we were in Montana
crossed the Powder River
the weather was growin' colder
men began to shiver

Winter coats were then unloaded
we never been so cold
we knew we wouldn't be up here
had all this been foretold

We began to see some wild bears
them grizzlies were the worst
whenever one come too near us
we shouted and then cursed

One old grizzly was the meanest
he must a' weighed a ton
that old 'teddy bear' was hungry
we thought it best to run

Our lead steer was a huge brindle
he wanted to go south
always tried to go his own way
and slobbered at the mouth

That critter meant to hold his ground
wantin' to fight that bear
when they charged at one another
it gave our broncs' a scare

Most of the boys were soon a'foot
or on some runaway
one cowboy came tearing' by us
screamin' to get away

That brindle was mad as could be
he pawed and charged that bear
the grizzly easily ripped off
'bout half the brindle's hair

The steer stopped and charged it again
and got a horn in him
they faced each other eyes a'fire
the fight was lookin' grim

Suddenly they both walked away
they settled with a draw
we gathered around the wagon
each in a state of awe

We came upon the Mussleshell
the river last to cross
we swam 'cross that ragin' river
scarin' even the boss

Abruptly Walter got startled
he slipped and fell away
then to our utter amazement
Jack jumped into the fray

That sad day the river took them
we stood in disbelief
my good friend and faithful partner
left me with so much grief

Next morning we held a service
our hats over our hearts
we put up a coupla' crosses
I'll gladly leave these parts

Three and a half cold days later
the river at our side
we came upon a high mesa
cow feed it would provide

We made camp late that afternoon
to rest a couple days
that night I lay and watched the stars
they're beauty did amaze

I was up at dawn next mornin'
hot coffee in my cup
I stood solemnly lookin' 'round
just cheerin' myself up

I looked out into the distance
a man was walking 'long
there behind him was a figure
the man whistlin' a song

As he drew nearer to our camp
I got a great surprise
that walk was oddly familiar
hard to believe my eyes

There was old Jack and young Walter
lookin' tired and restless
and with the biggest grin he said
"howdy, what's fer breakfast"?

This fable's finally over
the story is complete
Walter's still with us to this day
t'was never sold for meat

The Ballad of Bill Paxton
~~D. Weaver – ©2012 ~~

Into the town rode an outlaw, his gun was tied low at his hip.
The .44 was well cared for, and sported a bone handled grip.
He came here for a reason, hatred was on his unshaven face.
Said he was Clancy McDonald, and wouldn't be long at this place.

Old Willie Johnson was dozing, with his chair leaned back to the wall.
There in his lap was a puppy, gnawing on an old leather ball.
Old Willie had fallen asleep, his hand on his furry young friend.
Not one time thinking, the violence that was about to descend.

Clancy then strutted beside them, to enter the 'Wild Horse' saloon.
Savagely kicked their chair, and called each of them a mangy buffoon.
Willie's old seat crashed into pieces, and both were thrown to the floor.
Old Willie was then roughly hurtled, through the saloon's swinging door.

The puppy attacked Clancy quickly, meaning to tear him apart.
The outlaw drew his big .44, and shot him twice through his heart.
Some of the folks who had seen it, were shocked by the bloody display.
They turned away from the sight of it, each one going their own way.

The eyes of the outlaw then narrowed, he shouted out to the crowd.
I came to this town for vengeance, an oath to my father I've vowed.
Here lives a man I have searched for, I've wanted to kill him for years.
He shot my two older brothers, my family has shed many tears.

He didn't say how it had happened, strange how they often forget.
They had robbed a bank down in Waco, thinking no reason to fret.
On that day they met a young lawman, standing out there in the street.
He ordered them to surrender, but each one was filled with conceit.

Calmly again he warned them, they both felt he was out of his mind.
Both men went for their pistols, and his order was quickly declined.
The lawman proved to be faster, both went to Boot Hill in a box.
Their names are still standing up there, painted upon two slabs of rocks.

The folks living there in Waco, couldn't believe what they had seen.
Each of them watched in amazement, much too afraid to intervene.
The ranger did not fear them, he was simply enforcing the law.
They had never seen anyone like him, make that fast of a draw.

Bill Paxton was an ex-ranger, t'was known as the bravest and bold.
The stories about him were legends, but he was now growing old.
Bill was the fastest man ever, to pin on a ranger's tin star.
Most of the bad men all feared him, many of them carried Bill's scar.

Clancy's clothes were fancy and fitted, topped by a black leather vest.
Bragged of his bad reputation, his quickness he gladly professed.
Said he would leave us tomorrow, soon after the fighting was done.
He only rode in for pleasure, to see Old Bill under his gun.

Clancy said go send Bill a message, tell him a killer's in town.
I'm here to avenge my two brothers, soon you will be in the ground.
Hatred inside him was burning, he grinned like the devil possessed.
Old Bill replied with his answer, I'm coming to meet your request.

Some said it had been years now, since Bill Paxton had carried a gun.
Clancy bragged it wasn't his hide, just killing Old Bill would be fun.
Bill said I'll be there tomorrow, when the morning sun's coming up.
We can meet there in the street, this time you won't be facing a pup.

Bill rode in the next morning, the sun was hanging there in the sky.
In just a matter of minutes, the ranger or Clancy would die.
Slowly Bill slid from his saddle, Clancy waited there in the street.
The showdown was quickly approaching, each man was ready to meet.

Old Bill started talking to Clancy, judging the distance that way.
They stood apart at just thirty feet, and both men started their play.
Old Bill heard Clancy slap leather, knowing he was making his move.
Clancy McDonald would soon learn, his speed he needed to improve.

Bill's gun slipped leather like lightning, and his .44 had begun.
Six shots sent out a message, the old ranger had emptied his gun.
Each shot had found their target, they came flaming out one after one.
Bill then lowered his six-gun, knowing by the silence he had won.

Suddenly Clancy McDonald, stepped once and collapsed in the dirt.
Six holes were later discovered, stitched right across Clancy's new shirt.
Bill couldn't see Clancy's body, although it was clear in his mind.
The bright sun didn't bother him, because Old Bill Paxton was blind.

Bill has been gone for a long time, his legend we'll never forget.
Knowing this kind old ex-ranger, is one thing we'll never regret.
Some may not remember him, but the old-timers still can recall.
The day this old Texas Ranger, proved he was the bravest of all.

Brief Bios

Larry Bradfield was born in Southeastern New Mexico and grew up in West Texas during the oil boom in the Permian Basin. After retirement from the aerospace industry he started writing poetry that was descriptive of life growing up on the ranches of West Texas. He now lives with his beautiful wife, Joyce, in the Blue Ridge Mountains of North Georgia.

Clark Crouch is the prize-winning author of ten books of poetry, two of which (*Western Images* and *Views from the Saddle*) received the Will Rogers Medallion Award for cowboy poetry. Raised in Nebraska, he was influenced by a 1940s acquaintance with Badger Clark, who was then Poet Laureate of South Dakota, and has been writing and performing throughout the Northwest since 2002.

Neal Dachstadter was born in Georgia not too far from his family's Hereford and Angus farm. He lived in Albany, Texas and Reno, Nevada before deploying as a Chaplain to Hawijah with the Oregon, Idaho and Montana National Guard in 2005. After deployment he wrote full-time for 2 years on Lookout Mountain near Chattanooga. He then served as an Archivist, Chaplain and Teacher for Delta Kappa Epsilon in Ann Arbor for several years after. Neal is currently the "House Dad, Philosopher & Caretaker" of the Louisiana State Chapter of DKE in Baton Rouge.

Steve Dickson is a merchant seaman who was raised in the West. He previously worked in the lumber mills of Oregon and the big ranches of Texas, cooked at the Grand Canyon, and was a bouncer in Idaho and Washington. He hunted in the mountains and fished in the clear streams of Montana. He now resides in Grand Junction, Colorado with his lovely wife, Sandee, when not at sea.

Stephen Foster is the author of over 200 poems, most were written for and about family, so few have been offered for publication. Having grown up in Irving, Texas in a time when that part of Dallas county was considered rural, his writings are heavily influenced by the values of friends and relatives who grew up in the depression and post World War II era. His work in the Catholic church has led him to a closer relationship with God and a deep love for family and people in general. Current works reflect both family and spiritual influences.

Delia J. Fry plays the clarinet and alto saxophone. She has played with the O'Fallon concert and Jazz bands. She also writes and draws. Her writing has been featured in magazines, books, local newspapers and on poetry internet sites. Originally from Los Angeles, California, she has been living in Missouri for the past ten years.

Del Gustafson of Duvall, Washington was raised on a farm just south of the Canadian border. Some of his life experiences, including wild horse chases, have been documented in cowboy poems and his work has appeared in *Western Horseman, Open Range Magazine,* and on the web at CowboyPoetry.com.

Lynn Kopelke, AKA The Comic Cowboy of Cumberland, started out singing and playing guitar around campfires on both sides of the Cascade Mountains. He took his act to guest ranches and county fairs. Retirement centers to biker bars have enjoyed his blend of traditional, classic and contemporary cowboy music, original poetry, goofy humor, and really big hats. Lynn's thriving ragwort farm and cat ranch sits just two miles south of Cumberland, Washington. Stop on by.

Harold Losey, has been a resident of this "Blue Ball" since 1946 and seems to have weathered the time well. He was raised in an agricultural area in the mountains of northwestern New Jersey. In 1966 he joined the US Air Force where he spent the following 20+ years seeing parts of the world, but mostly Texas. He and his Texas wife raised two daughters, who gave them two wonderful granddaughters. He retired from the military in 1987 and has worked in the local North Texas school system since. He has had one book of poetry published (don't think it was read) and continues to write. In the last year or so trying his hand at a new genre, Western poetry.

Charli Love was raised on a cattle ranch in Jordan, Montana where she grew up in and around rodeo. Whether the family was moving cows or she was performing in the arena, she spent much of her time on the back of a horse. She still resides in the Big Sky State but now calls Bozeman home where she works as a cosmetologist. Her inspiration for writing poetry began when she heard Baxter Black in the poem "A Legacy of a Rodeo Man" featured in the movie *8 Seconds*. His words seemed to dance in perfect rhythm and she knew she wanted to write something like that.

Susan "S. D." Matley writes songs and poetry (published at cowboypoetry.com, Cowboys & Indians and From the Asylum). Her short stories have been published by *THEMA Literary Journal, GlassFire Magazine, Blade Red Press* and *Absent Willow Review*. Susan is currently working on a memoir-based novel, a western novel inspired by her Oregon pioneer great-great grandparents and a novella concerning the aftermath of the Whitman Massacre. She and husband Bruce are the cowboy music duo "Nevada Slim & Cimarron Sue". They live in Prescott, WA, amidst thousands of acres of wheat.

Debra G. Meyer of Greencastle, Indiana, wrote her first cowboy poem in 2007 after attending a cowboy gathering in Fort Worth, Texas. For the most part, Debra's poems are about the successes and misadventures of the eclectic group of folks who ride at Turning Point Equine Center, near Bainbridge, Indiana. Debra's poems have been published on cowboypoetry.com, westernpoetry.org, ropeandwire.com, and cowboypoetrypress.com. One of her poems, The Boots, was included in Western Poetry Publications' *Eight Viewpoints*, which was edited by Clark Crouch.

LTC Roy E. Peterson, a prolific author, has been published, not only as a western and cowboy poet, but in other genres as well. He is truly a multi-disciplined, multi-level author. Retired from the U.S. Army, he served in a number of military and civilian posts in Russia.

Tom Swearingen of Tualatin, Oregon, winner of the National Finals Rodeo 2013 Cowboy Poetry Week Contest, is a popular presenter at cowboy gatherings and wherever else you find folks who live and appreciate western heritage. Tom's poetry is often based on his own experiences, many of which occur as he and his wife ride their horses on Oregon's mountain trails. Tom's poems have been featured by *Cowboys & Indians Magazine* and cowboypoetry.com. His *Horses and Happiness* CD is available at oregoncowboypoet.com.

J. Wesley Taylor, Sr's. poetic works reflect his life and experience in the western United States. His employment with the U.S. Bureau of Land Management in Idaho and his out door experiences as a Scoutmaster, coupled with a family history of westward movement into Texas following the Civil War, have given him much grist for the poetic mill. Wes has published one chapbook, with a full length work now in progress.

Don Weaver was born in the San Joaguin Valley of California in 1945, the youngest of fourteen kids. He worked the fields and married at sixteen fifty years ago. He retired as a Captain in the Porterville Fire Department after going back to school. Began playing with poetry in 2009. Has to be inspired by a subject or person to write and loves funny poetry.

Made in the USA
Charleston, SC
27 July 2014